Origins

of

Huna

Secret Behind the Secret Science

Origins

of

Huna

Secret Behind the Secret Science

Shelley Kaehr, Ph.D.

Foreword by Raymond A. Moody, Jr., Ph.D., M.D.

FIRST EDITION
First Printing, 2002

Edited by Linnea M. Armstrong
Cover design by Michael Leone
Photos by Shelley Kaehr
Max Freedom Long photos property of Shelley Kaehr
William Tufts Brigham photo courtesy Bishop Museum

Library of Congress Control Number: 2002104081
Kaehr, Shelley A., 1967—
         Origins of huna : secret behind the secret science /
Shelley Kaehr — 1ˢᵗ ed.
              p.   cm.
              Includes bibliographical references.
              ISBN 0-9719340-0-2

An Out of This World Production does not participate in, endorse, or have any authority or responsibility concerning private business transactions between our authors and the public.

All mail addressed to the author is forwarded but the publisher cannot, unless specifically instructed by the author, give out an address or phone number.

If you wish to contact the author or would like more information about this book, please write to the author in care of An Out of This World Production and we will forward your request. Please write to:

Shelley Kaehr, Ph.D.
c/o An Out of This World Production
P.O. Box 610943
Dallas, TX 75261-0943

To Max
May he rest in peace.

Overleaf: Max Freedom Long, circa 1916
It is believed this photo was taken in California
prior to his departure to the Hawaiian Islands.

Acknowledgements

I am grateful to everyone who helped me bring this project to fruition. First and foremost, I thank my parents, Mickey and Gail and my brother Mark. Without their support, it would have taken me years longer to complete this task.

Special thanks to Jim Merideth who introduced me to Huna and who has helped me tremendously along my spiritual path.

There were numerous people in Hawaii who were invaluable to my research: Maile Meyer of Native Books, Pali Jae Lee, and April Drexel and Lilikala Kame'eleihiwa of the Hawaiian Studies Department of the University of Hawaii.

A huge "Mahalo" to Ron Schaeffer of the Bishop Museum—I so greatly appreciate everything you have done to help me! I also thank Pat Bacon, DeSoto Brown, Patty Lei Belcher, Janet Short and the rest of the staff of the Bishop Museum for all the wonderful things you do.

To Christine Cochrane and Kelly Rhoten, thank you for all your input in the early stages. You inspire me to always do my best. I also acknowledge my long time friend and editor for this project, Linnea M. Armstrong. I thank you for standing by my side all these years!

I am also grateful to the following individuals: Greg Stephens, Mike Reynolds, April Reckling, Elizabeth Ringham Cruz, Ana Towry, Joan Scott Lowe and especially all of my clients for sharing your stories and opening your hearts.

Finally, sincere thanks to Dr. Raymond Moody for his support and encouragement. My life has been so heavily influenced by his work in *Life After Life*, the very first book I ever read on paranormal topics at age nine. I am proud to call him my friend.

Table of Contents
Part 1

Part 2
Discovering the Secret of Huna

"It is vitally important that we gain
the right understanding of things
here, for when we die and cross into
the after-life in the shadowy bodies,
the things we have believed here
become almost fixations,
and may haunt us there."

Max Freedom Long

Foreword

Shelley Kaehr's *Origins of Huna* is a truly special piece of work for it shows an admirable desire to get to the truth. And, regrettably, this is a quality that is lacking in many works about spiritual matters.

Specifically, many people subscribe to the teachings of professed gurus and spiritual masters that later turn out to be bogus. Once the facts come out, disappointed followers tend to behave in one of two contrasting ways. They may refuse to face the facts, become even more devoted to the guru, and flee from reality into a cult, or they may become embittered and cynical about all spiritual teachings whatsoever.

Shelley's reaction was entirely atypical. Without hesitation, she owned up to the truth about a bogus doctrine with which she had become. Then, she wrote this most interesting book in which she reports the startling results of her search for the truth about the doctrine. And she does so in a straightforward manner with no bitterness or recriminations.

Since the belief system with which she was involved—Huna—has spread to so many people, her book is timely and important. I recommend it to all who are deeply interested in paranormal phenomena, alternative medicine, and New Age spiritual movements, and I commend Shelley for her heartfelt commitment to the spirit of honest inquiry.

Raymond A. Moody, Jr., M.D.

Introduction

After studying Huna for nearly a year, I was continually puzzled by questions people would ask about it. What exactly is Huna, where did it originate, what can it do, and why? Is it merely a form of Wicca, as suggested by Raymond Buckland in his book, *Buckland's Complete Book of Witchcraft*, or is it actually a true representation of the ancient religion of Polynesia?

When I began this project over two years ago, I truly did not know the answers to these questions myself, and I must admit that as I began doing this research, I was literally stunned by much of the information I found.

What I thought would be a simple answer to a question has turned up more and more questions— many of which may never be adequately answered. My hope is that I may present what I have discovered in such a way so that the reader may know my opinion and also be able to draw his or her own conclusions about an extremely complex subject.

In my private practice, I have been able to use many of the teachings of what I had known to be Huna with very positive results. I have discovered from this research, however, that there was much I did not know about Huna and that, as in all things in life, things are never what they appear to be.

Any type of spiritual teaching is bound to have gray areas which one may ponder without ever really knowing the truth. This is one such study.

My goal for the reader is threefold. First, I hope to facilitate a better understanding of this obscure teaching. Second, I hope the reader will acquire knowledge about the fundamentals of Huna. Last—and most importantly—I want to dispel some of the misrepresentations and misconceptions held by the public about the origins of Huna.

One
How it All Began

People are always curious about how I got into studying Huna and why I have devoted so much time to this research. The answer is simple: I fell into it.

The way this project has unfolded over the past couple of years has been quite amazing and almost magical to me, which is why I wonder if I am totally in charge here. I believe we all want to work doing things we enjoy and hope to find the inner peace that can only come from following one's life's purpose. It is difficult for most of us to finally reach the point when we figure out what it is we are to do with our life.

The way this work has come together for me and the exciting journey I have been on to discover what I have so far, has left me with a feeling of satisfaction that indeed I am on my way to figuring out some kind of meaning in my life. This research is certainly a big part of my journey, and a challenging one at that.

I was living in Colorado when I first learned of Huna through a friend who had studied with a teacher in Dallas, Texas. He suggested I check out various websites on the subject because he believed this was a system that truly had *the answer* to the universal question: What is the meaning of life? I was also told this was the teaching of the twelve tribes of Israel; I must admit captured my attention rather quickly. I read some of the information about Huna that was available at the time on the Internet, but was distracted at the time with a pending divorce.

Despite this distraction, my intuitive voice was developing rapidly and I was learning to truly tune in to my inner guidance in a way I had not before. At the time, I was understandably going through a wicked bout of depression when one afternoon the "little voice in my head" (I often joke by telling people I am not schizophrenic!) told me there was something wrong with my heart and I would not live much longer. This was an alarming announcement and whether it was true, or became a self-fulfilling prophecy, I will never know.

What I do know is during the night, I went to sleep and was awakened by the feeling of my soul being torn from my body. It was more than a mere out-of-body experience. This felt like I was leaving and not coming back. I saw a glowing light in front of me and I reached down and felt my heart and realized it was barely beating. I stood up and walked to the window and recall looking out at the full moon wondering if this was really the end for me. Maybe it was time and I was about to check out. I felt okay with it.

I went back to bed after allowing my heartbeat to stabilize and began to go to sleep when it happened again. Suddenly the "fight or flight" response kicked in and I decided to fight. I called my neighbor across the hall who came over and was trying not to look pan-icked as he attempted to find my pulse. I could see the fear in his eyes, though his voice was calm as he said, "We need to go to the hospital."

By the time I arrived, my pulse was in the low 30's

and I stayed hooked up to monitors throughout the night. The final analysis remains a mystery: the doctors said I must have been ill with a virus. There was no other explanation. They had to reach some conclusion.

Was I attempting to commit a form of psychic suicide by simply willing myself to die? There is no way to know at this point, but I feel it must be something like that. Regardless of what it was, I do know I was never the same after that night.

I came back to Dallas the next week and found that from time to time I would find myself going somewhere in between worlds—as if I was in a space between life and death. That is the only way I can explain it. I continued to feel my heart grow weak at times and often saw the tunnel of white light people describe in books. I wondered if I could hang on, or if I was getting ready to leave.

It was then that my friend showed me what he knew about Huna. He used some powerful Huna energy on me to literally "put me back together" again. I felt my soul reconnect with my body and it stayed put.

The combination of this, with a series of powerful past-life regressions helped me in a way I felt was phenomenal. I was now a believer of Huna, and was anxious to find out more.

I enrolled in the Huna course in Dallas – the same one my friend had taken. I found it to be somewhat enlightening; however, I seemed to never be able to get a straight answer about Huna. I could never define it in a way that I felt was satisfactory. I felt I was a person of at least reasonable intelligence, yet I could never quite understand why I could not comprehend the meaning of the term Huna. I wanted an exact definition of it so I would be able to tell other people about it and spread the word. I left the course confused and several thousand dollars lighter.

After my strange near-death experience, I began to notice that I had somehow developed a strong healing ability of my own. I instantaneously seemed to know how to heal and exactly what to do simply by laying hands on myself. I knew that someday I would be doing this type of work on others. I also used the Huna style of work I had learned in my class, and it seemed to have amazing results.

Two
Someone Pays a Visit

That experience led me on a journey to finish my
Ph.D. I was persuaded to write my dissertation on
Huna, primarily to help the people at my school understand it because nobody in the Parapsychic Science
program had ever written on the subject before. As a
practicing hypnotherapist specializing in past-life
regressions, I was actually much more interested in
relaying accounts and theories on reincarnation than in
writing about the study of Huna, but decided to do the
work anyway.

The first question I asked in my research was why
was I having trouble finding any native Hawaiians to
speak to about Huna?

The next question that puzzled me was why, after
reading literally everything in print on the subject of
Huna, was it that the healing symbols I learned in class
were only mentioned in one book written by the person
who introduced them to the world?

These things seemed strange to me, and the
questions led me on a path of discovery about the true
origins of Huna.

As I was working on the writing and research, I
began to sense a presence around me in my home.
Each night I would hear a banging noise as if someone

were rapping on one of the pictures on the wall near my bed. I had been visited before by departed loved ones, so after ruling out every ordinary possibility, I began to accept that a spirit was visiting me.

The question was who, and why were they visiting now? Having studied many paranormal matters, I am under the belief system that one does not come from beyond the grave unless they are in need of some kind of healing.

I had no idea who it was or what I could possibly do to help, but figured at some point I would have to find out.

The noises continued every evening becoming more persistent and annoying. I did all I could to ignore the loud rapping for as long as possible. I went on vacation and assumed whatever it was would be gone when I returned so I would not have to deal with it. Of course, that was not the case, and after my return the knocking became even louder, more frequent, and much more persistent.

I began to have "thoughts" that this spirit would like me to take its picture. I thought this seemed a bit ridiculous, but felt that if I should capture anything on film, it would only prove that the sounds I was hearing were real and not just figments of my imagination.

I enjoy watching documentaries on Discovery Channel where the real-life ghostbusters use various types of equipment to capture the orbs of light in supposedly haunted rooms. I had previously picked up images on film that I felt were apparitions, so I assumed this would be no different.

The evening I decided to try my experiment, I accidentally went to bed without the camera anywhere near me. Immediately after I shut off the light, the rapping began, and it was louder than ever before. I knew whoever it was meant business, and was ready for me to acknowledge its presence. I jumped from my bed and ran downstairs to get the camera and loaded it up. By "coincidence" (I say this sarcastically, as I do not believe anything happens by accident), I happened to have a roll of high-speed film. I loaded it and ran upstairs. "Okay, if you want to be known, just appear on my film!" I said as I began to take shots in the pitch dark.

Sure enough, the film showed the presence of something abnormal. It was enough to convince me that someone, or something, was there who definitely wanted its presence known.

That night, I was able to capture on film what looked like concentrated orbs that formed an outline that vaguely resembled the shape of a person. The figure was standing in one spot in the room. It was compelling enough to make me feel I was indeed being visited.

Next, the "thought" came into my mind that I should get a Ouija Board and talk to this person.

I immediately declined, thinking this was a ludicrous idea, and absolutely refused to take part in such things. I had one when I was a child and had scared myself to death with it while playing with friends. In particular, reading the book *Ghost of Flight 401* where people communicated with dead spirits from a plane crash using a Ouija Board, then watching the television movie based on the book scared me half to death. I threw the board in the trash, vowing never to own one again.

Over the years, I developed the idea that Ouija Boards were wrong and let in all sorts of dark energies.

Getting one at that point was not an option for me at all!

Sure enough, that same day my friend who had introduced me to Huna called to tell me about going to a medium and how beneficial it was because they had used a Ouija Board. He explained a process by which the medium surrounded himself in white light so it was all very safe and extremely effective.

I could simply not ignore the timing of his message. Assuming this was some sort of indirect communication from beyond, I gave in, and became convinced to try it.

I went out and looked for a board and was a bit surprised to find one at the local Wal-Mart. I was somewhat shocked that the conservative population had not dissuaded them from carrying it. Now my only challenge was figuring out who would I get to try this with me. I knew my brother would be game so I told him about the plan.

We set the time for midnight, and sat up with my newly acquired Ouija Board to begin the process of attempting to communicate with the dead.

Initially, the communication came in very slowly, and was extremely choppy, as if it were in code. None of the letters seemed to fit or spell much of anything and the signal did not seem to be very strong. The longer the session went, though, the more I realized a strengthening of presence and energy and diligently transcribed the letters one by one.

At first glance, when all the letters were out in the open, I could not make heads nor tails of their meaning. It all seemed like a chaotic mess. After staring for a few seconds at the jumbled letters with literally no clue as to who this might be, I suddenly deciphered the meaning and my mouth fell open at the discovery. Here is what my transcript said:

IMDRLNGMXFREDOMIAMABIGKAHUNA
(I am Dr. Long, Max Freedom. I am a Big Kahuna)

I was completely in shock by this and had a hard time accepting it at first. I soon verified it by asking "Dr. Long" questions relating to a number of personal details including age at death, birth year, birthplace, etc., which I was able to confirm later in my research.

My main question was: Why me? What is your purpose in coming here now? After all, what could I possibly have to offer, I asked the board and myself? The answer he gave puzzled me at first, but as I continued with my research I eventually came to understand the full meaning of it: BECAUSE GOD TOLD ME TO was the answer spelled out.

As the line of communication strengthened, the Ouija Board quickly became obsolete and was replaced by a pen and paper in a journal and next by the keys of my computer, thus beginning my work as an automatic writer. I had been trying to do automatic writing for years with absolutely no success. Suddenly what had once seemed to be such a struggle was now completely effortless.

For the next several months I had conversations with Max nearly every day and much of the research and the conclusions I have been led to are directly guided by him.

With the help of my new discarnate friend, I was led on an amazing adventure to finally unravel some of the hidden secrets of Huna, as told by the man who invented the system himself-Max Freedom Long.

Three
The Hawaiian Culture

In order to adequately describe Huna in its entire context, I feel it will be helpful to provide the reader with a brief description of the Hawaiian culture and the history of the most geographically isolated landmasses in the world.

Hawaii literally means "breath and water," referring to two of the basic premises behind Huna. Situated in the area that is now speculated to be the remains of the lost civilization of Lemuria, the islands are rich with spirituality and cultural heritage.

Hawaiians worshipped several deities, who represented various things in the physical environment. Each was depicted by various natural phenomenon called *kinolau*. According to the *Hawaiian Dictionary*, *kinolau* means "many forms taken by a supernatural, such as Pele." In other words, when we see certain things out in nature such as sugarcane, the Hawaiian people would say that *is* the god Kane.

There are literally over 40,000 gods and goddesses in the Hawaiian culture. For this writing I will primarily concentrate on the major deities, and will include a discussion of lesser gods in Part 2 of the book.

There were four main gods: Kane, Ku, Lono and Kanaloa, each of which symbolized one of the four parts of man according to Huna.

Kane represented the *'aumakua*, or higher self, in Huna. He was seen as vital force. His *kinolau*, or outer manifestations, included sugarcane, the sun, fresh water, winds, and the albatross.

Ku was the symbol of man's *unihipili*, or unconscious mind, in Huna. He was the Hawaiian god of war to whom human sacrifices were occasionally made. Symbolized by the morning sun, Ku was often seen as the hawk, the eel, or as coconuts.

Lono, god of peace, provided food for the people of the islands. In Huna, he was the symbol for the *uhane*, or conscious mind of the person. He had several *kinolau*, including the pig and many of the native fish. A fruitful harvest was a sign that Lono had blessed the islands. Because he was seen as provider, he was much revered and loved by the people.

The last of the major gods was Kanaloa. Symbolized by the physical body in Huna, he was the god of the ocean. He was not typically as well-known, but gained notoriety by being the companion to Kane. When Christian missionaries arrived on the islands, many mistakenly believed that Kanaloa was Satan. His *kinolau* included the water and all marine life forms including the fish, octopus, as well as the ocean itself.

Goddesses were not as prevalent in Hawaii with one exception–Pele, goddess of the Volcano of Kilauea on the island of Hawaii. The most popular deity in modern times, she is associated with both creation and destruction. Several myths continue to this day concerning Pele, as she is often noted to present herself in human form.

One urban legend recounts several incidents in which people were driving along the highway, saw a

Ancient Hawaiian Deities

Gods

	Spiritual Significance	Elements	Animals	Offerings	Color	Kinolau
Kane	Life force, procreation and fertility	sun, fresh water, wind	albatross	awa, pigs, bark	yellow	sugar cane
Ku	God of war, fighting, agriculture forests, canoes, some sorcery	morning sun	hawk, eel, sea cucumber	human sacrifice	red	coconut, breadfruit
Lono	Peace, provider of food, sports - bowling, boxing, wrestling, sledding running, agriculture	clouds, wind, rain, thunder, storms, whirlwinds, waterspouts gushing springs	pig, many fish	coconuts, sweet potatoes, feathers	red black	fruitful harvests
Kanaloa	Companion to Kane, god of the sea smooth sailing, protection at sea	water - tides, sea, fish ponds	mullet and other fish, octopus/squid	awa, whitefish, pigs	white	bananas

Goddesses

	Spiritual Significance	Elements	Animals	Offerings	Color	Kinolau
Pele	Volcano Kilauea, destruction, creation, linked with Lono	fire, thunder	none	awa, pig, hair, fruit flowers, gin, coins, incense, berries	red black	human, flame young or old woman
Laka	Hula and forest plants	earth	none	awa, fruit	yellow	Hula dance
Haumea	Earth mother, childbirth, mother of Pele, creator of the Hawaiian people	earth	none	breadfruit	red	assumed many human forms-young and old
Hina	Goddess of the moon, linked with Ku medicinal herbs	air, water	corals and spiny sea creatures	fish	white	coral reef, seaweed, forests

33

beautiful young woman with long wavy black hair, and offered her a ride. Shortly after getting in the car,

the woman somehow disappeared. Pele's other *kinolau* include her manifestation as a very old woman, or as any form of fire.

There is also much superstition surrounding the volcanoes on the islands. It is said that Pele is deeply angered when anyone dare to remove any of the volcanic rocks from her home. These people are supposedly "cursed" and become subject to great misfortune. As they begin to realize the cause of their ailments, they often return the sand or rocks. The Hawaiian government claims to receive several hundred boxes of lava per year.

The other most famous goddesses include Laka, to whom the Hula dance is attributed; Hi'aka, sister to Pele; Hina, goddess of the moon and mother to demigod Maui; and Haumea, who is the mother of all Hawaiians.

The deities enjoyed various offerings, one of the favorites being the special drink *awa*, a kava-kava tea. This kava-kava, however, is certainly not at all like anything we encounter in our herbal teas on the mainland. The kava is pure in form, and can be extremely intoxicating. Despite its potency, it is not considered an alcoholic beverage and is enjoyed by many Hawaiians to this day. It is highly relaxing and is supposedly used to achieve greater altered states in meditation.

One interesting note is that in December 2001 the Food and Drug Administration sent out a letter to healthcare professionals in the U.S. with a warning about kava, citing a potential link between the use of this herb and diseases of the liver, including hepatitis, cirrhosis and liver failure. The problem has raised such concerns overseas that the Swiss government recently banned its use. This has upset many Huna practitioners in the States who enjoy using the concentrated Polynesian version of this relaxing herb.

There are four main spiritual colors in Hawaii: red, yellow, white and black. Each god or goddess resonated to at least one of these. Unlike the European culture, in which black is seen as a negative, in Hawaii black was a very positive color. It was the color of Lono, and represented the volcanic earth from which crops and food originated. Also associated with volcanoes and the rich lava that flowed from them was the color red, which was dedicated to the god Ku because it was the color of blood. It could also symbolize Lono for the redfish offered to him, or the hair of the goddess Pele. Yellow represents the sun, or life force, and is symbolized by the god Kane. Yellow was the sacred color of the *ali'i*, or ruling class, and was also used by the goddess Laka. To this day, one can see statues of King Kamehameha I clothed in yellow. White is also a color sacred to Hawaiians. Many of the prayer priests, or *kahuna pule*, wore white robes in religious ceremonies. White could also be seen in the clouds, ocean, or in the snow on top of Mauna Kea on the island of Hawaii.

Overall, the Hawaiian culture is rich in mythology and lore, much of which will be discussed in greater detail throughout the book.

.

Four
Brief History of Hawaii

It is believed that the islands now known as Hawaii were first inhabited by Polynesians who arrived in outrigger canoes sometime in the first millennium A.D. Most scholars specifically accept 500-700 A.D. as the time frame for this occurrence. It is speculated that the immigrants settled first upon the shores of the island of Molokai. Many scholars now believe these first settlers came from a small island near Tahiti called Havaii, which is substantiated by the name of the Kealaikahiki Channel between the islands of Lanai and Kaho'olawe, which translates to "The way to Tahiti."

Pa'ao

Sometime around 1175, the man who was to have perhaps the greatest influence on the islands—a Tahitian priest known as Pa'ao—arrived in Hawaii.

We now know of the existence of Pa'ao because of references made to him in ancient Hawaiian chants. He was supposedly a white man and was responsible for bringing much of the idolatry to the islands in the form of wooden statues erected to the gods. Scholars now believe he may have actually been a Catholic priest.

Legend says that Pa'ao was living in Tahiti with his family when his brother accused Pa'ao's son of stealing fruit from him, which was considered to be a sin.

The boy denied the accusations and told his uncle he would gladly prove he did not commit the crime by allowing his stomach to be cut open so it may be searched for remnants of the stolen fruit.

The test was given and the boy passed. He did not steal the fruit; however, the procedure cost him his life.

A furious and grief-stricken Pa'ao decided to leave Tahiti and travel to a new locale. Before he left, he had his brother's son killed and hid his body underneath his ship so the deed would not be discovered until after he had set sail.

Many of Pa'ao's followers wanted to accompany him to his new home and he agreed to let them if they could "fly" onto the ship from the cliffs surrounding the harbor. Many tried to leap and lost their lives, a few made it, and many others were left behind to endure the wrath of the angry new ruler. Pa'ao came to the islands and erected many statues and temples to worship the gods. Cross-like artifacts that have been found have led to the belief he may have been Catholic.

Pa'ao was the first to institute the human sacrifice. It has been confirmed that sacrifices were made at Mo'okini *Heiau* on the Big Island of Hawaii. A *heiau* is a pre-Christian place of worship. Contrary to popular belief, however, human sacrifices were rare in ancient Hawaii.

Many wanted Pa'ao to become the king. He declined and brought another powerful man named Pili from Tahiti to serve as ruler of the islands. Instead,

Pa'ao became the first in the long and infamous line of *kahuna* known as the lineage of *kahuna nui*.

Pili was the direct lineage of many of the greatest kings of Hawaii, including the line of Kamehamehas. This began the monarchy system of government in the islands.

Because of the geographic isolation of the islands, disease was virtually unknown at this time, and the Hawaiians flourished in beautiful surroundings, isolated from the rest of the world.

The Arrival of Cook

In 1778, all of that changed. The famous British naval officer Captain James Cook accidentally discovered Hawaii while on an expedition for the British Navy to attempt to find a Northwest Passage from the Pacific to the Atlantic oceans.

Was Cook actually the very first person from the outside world to discover these islands? There is truly no way to know this with absolute certainty, although he was definitely the first to leave traces of his presence there.

Cook's ship landed at Waimea on the island of Kauai. After proclaiming his newfound discovery a British territory, he named Hawaii the "Sandwich Islands," after a British Earl.

For the Hawaiian people, the arrival of Captain Cook was seen as a prophecy come true. It had been foretold that the god Lono would return via a floating island. The natives had never before seen the white man, and certainly had never seen ships, which were mistaken for floating islands.

Obviously the Hawaiians concluded Cook was their god in the flesh. They generously bestowed many offerings to Cook and his crew, which were foolishly accepted. Cook enjoyed the pampering and attention he was receiving. As the truth of Cook's identity eventually began to surface, however, arguments broke out which ultimately cost him his life.

Captain Cook's final blow happened when he was accidentally wounded and began to bleed. When the Hawaiians saw their "god" was bleeding like a mere mortal, they were deeply offended; Cook was shot dead in the water of Kealeakua Bay off the island of Hawaii.

To this day, British naval ships stop in Kealeakua Bay annually to pay homage to the great seafarer. In addition, there are many towns and monuments dedicated to Cook throughout the islands.

At that time, each island was ruled by a separate monarch until 1810 when King Kamehameha I united all of the islands.

Captain Cook statue on Kauai

Kamehameha The Great

Kamehameha, "the lonely one", as he was called, is an extremely important part of Hawaiian history and culture.

It is speculated he was born in 1758 in the northern part of Hawaii in the Kohala District. Some scholars believe he was the son of Chief Keoua, the half brother of King Kalaniopuu; others claim he was the son of a great Maui war chief named Kahekili.

Kamehameha was born and lived much of his life prior to the arrival of the white man to the islands. In 1775, he overturned the famous Naha Stone (weighing over 5,000 pounds). It was prophesied that he who overturns the stone would conquer all the islands, which is exactly what he did.

Kamehameha I ruled half the island of Hawaii. After successful campaigns in Maui, Lanai and Molokai and a battle in Oahu, Kamehameha ruled the majority of the islands by the year 1791. Finally in 1810, the ruler of Ni'ihau and Kauai ceded power to Kamehameha, thus uniting all islands under a single rule.

Part of Kamehameha's success in this endeavor was due to the fact that he was able to befriend the white visitors and learn much from them, including how to use their weapons against the weaker opposition of the other local rulers.

In 1818, Kamehameha I protested the British name "Sandwich Islands," and proposed that each island be given its own name and that they should collectively be called the "Islands of The Kingdom of Hawaii."

The culture during Kamehameha's reign was rich with spirituality and deeply rooted with a love and respect for the gods and goddesses, which were represented throughout the natural world. The native people practiced a mysterious form of magic through their priests, or *kahuna*. The word *kahuna* literally means "expert" in Hawaiian, and there are many types of *kahuna*. Similar to many other cultures, in ancient Hawaii professions were often chosen for people prior to, or shortly after their birth. Someone could be born a toolmaker, farmer, or any other profession, and that person would serve a form of apprenticeship.

After completing the study, the person would be called a "*kahuna*," or expert. It would be similar to having a Ph.D. in our modern day terms.

Of course, for the intent of this discussion, when we speak of *kahuna*, we are talking about the spiritual leaders of the people – the priests. In Part 2, I will describe some of the other types of *kahuna* prevalent in ancient Hawaii.

King Kamehameha The Great

Hewahewa Changes History

During the reign of Kamehameha I, the monarch relied heavily on the advice of the most powerful *kahuna* of the time, Hewahewa, a direct descendent of Pa'ao.

Shortly after Kamehameha's death in May 1819, Hewahewa began to use his psychic abilities to see into the future. He had a vision of the pending arrival of the missionaries to Hawaii.

Hewahewa sensed that these visitors would bring some type of spiritual enlightenment with them, imagined that this would be a great event in the history of the islands, and was curious to see if anyone could indoctrinate him to the religion of the white man.

Hewahewa saw his vision as a "sign" from the gods, and began to question the white British naval officers about their religious beliefs. They told him stories of Jesus, and how he performed miraculous healings and rose from the dead in three days.

Hewahewa was deeply impressed and felt that because of the power of Jesus that these white men must also possess great healing power—perhaps even greater than that of the island *kahuna*.

In an effort to secure his own power and to be able to fall into the good graces of the pending visitors, Hewahewa proceeded to have all of the *kahuna* executed and many of the temples of the gods destroyed prior to the arrival of the missionaries.

In April 1820, as he predicted, the first Christian missionaries arrived on the exact beach he had foreseen the previous year.

The first group, or company, of missionaries left Boston on October 23, 1819, and arrived on April 4,

1820, anchoring in Kailua Bay on the island of Hawaii.

The group brought members of many professions with them, including ministers, physicians, teachers, printers, bookbinders, and farmers.

Upon arrival, the missionaries concluded the Hawaiian people had lost faith in their own religious system, after seeing the desecrated temples with their own eyes.

Liholiho Creates Greater Women's Rights

The other contributing factor to their opinion was the fact that Kamehameha's son, Liholiho, who was now Kamehameha II, had abolished many of the ancient taboos set forth in the old religion. He altered what he considered to be outdated ancient customs by allowing women to eat at the same tables as men.

Liholiho completely threw out the ancient *kapu*, or taboo system. With it, many of the old ways were forever changed, ultimately for the better. Many of the *kapu* were set to restrict the activities of women. Scholars now speculate that men in that time found women threatening due to their reproductive and intuitive capabilities. Liholiho's actions paved the way for greater equality for women.

Meanwhile, Hewahewa was very pleased with himself and what he considered to be his accurate predictions about the new arrivals to the islands. He quickly brought all of the ill and infirm to the mission-aries to see the miracles he thought they could perform, and was sorely dissappointed to learn the new arrivals could not heal anyone. The blind remained blind, the ill and infirm left unhealed. Hewahewa discovered that the now nearly extinct *kahuna* had actually been much more powerful than he originally imagined.

Hopeful that he may have been mistaken, Hewahewa continued to aid the missionaries by feeding them, befriending them, and helping them build temples.

Once the temples were constructed, his new friends wanted Hewahewa to convert to Christianity; when he refused, they quickly dissociated themselves from him.

As the missionaries became more established and converted more native people to Christianity, they quickly gained control of the population through their wealth and affluence. Soon all forms of Hawaiian ritual were outlawed, and remained so until the late 1900s.

Lot Kapuaiwa Kamehameha V

The last monarch in the Kamehameha lineage was King Lot, who had a tremendous impact on the spiritual practices of the native people.

Lot ruled from 1863-1872, and wanted to increase the power of the monarchy, so he refused to abide by the constitution of 1852 and proceeded to have it changed.

In the new 1864 Constitution of Hawaii, Lot succeeded in getting everything he wanted. First, there would no longer be an office of *Kuhina Hui*, or co-ruler of the kingdom. Lot no longer wanted to share the reign with his sister, Princess Victoria. Second, he succeeded in limiting the power of the privy council, which was set up as a checks and balances system for the king. By limiting their power, he garnered more for himself. Last, he decided voters must be literate and own property. Previously the right was granted to any man over 25 years in age.

It was also during the reign of King Lot that leprosy began to take over the islands. It was he who made the decision to confine those inflicted with the disease to the remote shores of Molokai, a painful and heart-breaking chapter in Hawaiian history.

As far as spiritual practices were concerned, Lot was the first to attempt to control and regulate the profession of *kahuna*. Law would now require all *kahuna* to become registered, and by doing so, they would be issued certificates so they would be allowed to practice native medicine. According to the July 1892 issue of *The Friend*, a missionary newspaper, there were some 300 *kahuna* licensed at that time. Some feel this was a strictly political move on the part of King Lot, who was interested in gaining favor amongst the powerful missionary settlers at the time. Regardless of his motivation, it hurt the Hawaiian people the most by placing native practices under even greater scrutiny than they already were.

Iolani Palace in Honolulu

The End of the Monarchy

After the sudden death of King Lot in 1872, an election was held for the first time to determine the future monarch. Lunalilo was selected and ruled only a year until he died suddenly and was succeeded by King David Kalakaua, the "Merry Monarch," in 1874. Kalakaua was responsible for building the famed Iolani Palace in Honolulu, the only royal palace in the United States, which was completed in 1882.

Kalakaua was the first Hawaiian monarch to tour the world. The beloved ruler was responsible for legalizing the Hula dance, and publishing a well-received collection of Hawaiian stories called *The Legends and Myths of Hawaii*. On a trip to San Francisco in 1891, Kalakaua died, leaving the throne to his sister, Queen Liliuokalani, who would be the last reigning monarch of the Kingdom of Hawaii. Liliuokalani is most remembered for writing the famous song "Aloha Oe."

In 1893, the Queen was overthrown and a temporary government was established under Stanford B. Dole, who became the first president of Hawaii in 1894, and remained in that position until the United States annexed Hawaii on August 12, 1898.

Spiritual Practices Finally Legalized

The first law passed to help restore Hawaii's native culture was the American Indian Religious Freedom Act of 1978, which enabled all Native Americans, including the Hawaiians, "to believe, express, and exercise their traditional religions." It also allowed the

Hawaiian people to have *"access to (sacred) sites, use and possession of sacred objects, and the freedom to worship through ceremonial and traditional rites."*

This was the first of many laws passed to right the wrongs done to native cultures. These issues are still pressing today and are of major concern to the cultural Hawaiians, as well as other Native American groups.

Five
How Huna was Started

In 1917, a young American man named Max Freedom Long went to Hawaii to teach. Long was born in Sterling, Colorado, on October 26, 1890. He lived in Denver for several years before moving to southern California where he received a BA in General Studies from UCLA on June 22, 1916.

Long was interested in photography, which may have been the reason teaching in the Hawaiian Islands appealed to him.

Soon after his arrival in Hawaii, Long became curious about the various cultural secrets of the native people, and began to inquire about the *kahuna* and the ancient magic.

Long, a skeptic who said he did not believe in such things as magic, wanted to prove that the stories he had heard about the native Shamanism were myths.

His inquiries were not welcomed at all by the local people and every lead he found concerning the old ways turned out to be nothing. This puzzled Long and he persistently continued seeking the truth.

In his third year on the islands, Long said he became the tenant of a Hawaiian woman who was a self-ordained minister practicing rituals based on the ancient teachings. Although he seemed to make a bit of progress in his quest, the people were unwilling to share much with Long other than what he happened to observe in passing, primarily due to the fact that at the time it was illegal to discuss such matters in public. To do so could have resulted in steep fines and/or imprisonment.

After four years on the islands, Long said he befriended the long-time curator of the Bishop Museum in Honolulu, Dr. William Tufts Brigham, who confidentially told him about many magical acts and rituals he said he had witnessed and performed in his 40 years on the islands.

Long said Brigham's dilemma was that he could not figure out the secret that enabled the magic to happen, and he had devoted much of his life attempting to answer that question.

According to Long's most noted book, *The Secret Science Behind Miracles*, four years after their first meeting, Brigham died, and left Long with the task of completing his life's work – to crack the ancient code of the *kahuna* and discover the key to their longevity. Long explained that he was so fascinated by the beliefs supposedly held by this respected scientist, he felt he had an obligation to complete the work.

Long left Hawaii in 1931 and moved back to California, where in 1935 he said he had a dream in which the answer came to him. The code must be buried in the Hawaiian language!

Long began to dissect the ancient chants and analyze the hidden meanings in the roots of the words. This was a difficult task due to the fact that the Hawaiian language only has seven consonants, unlike English, which has 21. What this implies is that the language is extremely ambiguous, and therefore, one word has many meanings.

After years of research, Long felt he had discovered all he could, and published his first book, *Recovering the Ancient Magic*, in 1936. In this first writing, Long said he put out a call to anyone who may have any information to share on further insights into the mystery.

After a year, he said he received a letter from a man named Reginald Stewart, a British journalist who had traveled into Africa and befriended members of a local tribe, the Berbers, located in the Atlas Mountains in the northern part of the continent. Stewart recognized the Hawaiian words as being strikingly similar to the language he encountered in Africa, and decided to write Long to tell his story.

Apparently, while in Africa, Stewart stumbled across the Berbers, and somehow talked the tribal priestess into teaching him the ancient secrets. The woman was already preparing to teach the lore to her grandaughter, so she agreed to allow him to work with them.

According to Long, the woman told Stewart that the ancient teachings began in the Sahara Desert until it became barren, at which time the tribe moved into the area near the Nile in ancient Egypt. From there, the tribes separated and all but hers went North toward India.

Unfortunately, this was about all the priestess related to Stewart, because in a freak accident, she was supposedly shot by a stray bullet and fell dead in front of him. Long explained that she carried the secrets of the magic with her to the grave, much to Stewart's dismay.

The alleged testimony of Stewart and the extensive

research that followed led Long to believe that the ancient secret of the *kahuna* must have originated in Africa before spreading to India, Tibet, China, and Polynesia before finally reaching Hawaii.

In addition, Long believed there were 11 tribes of ancient Polynesians who inhabited many different islands, including New Zealand, Samoa and Taiwan. Each carried a unique dialect. Long said his research "proves" that of all the original Polynesian tribes, it was only those who settled in Hawaii who kept the language in its purest form.

Long said this was partly due to the cultural leaders' demand that the language be kept pure. For example, Long believed that *kahuna* priests-in-training were dismissed from their calling if they dared mispronounce any words. That fact combined with the geographic isolation of the area allowed the language to remain, according to Long, virtually untouched and true to its original form.

Therefore, in Long's opinion, if one wanted to gain true insight into the ancient secrets, it is best done using the Hawaiian dialect rather than what he called the other more tainted versions of the Polynesian language.

Long also conducted exhaustive research in an attempt to "prove" that Jesus was a *kahuna*, and that many of the parables of the four Gospels are directly related to the inner teachings of the secret religion. Long wrote several books on this subject, including *Huna Code in Religions* and *What Jesus Taught in Secret*.

In these works, Long references many elements of what he calls the "hidden language" used to attempt to keep the teachings of Jesus alive through parables.

Long felt Paul's dogmatic interpretation of the New Testament was to blame for many of the teachings falling on the deaf ears of Christians who chose to interpret the Bible literally, instead of searching for the hidden meanings found riddled in the text.

On a similar note for those who have studied Reiki, the healing system of Japan, Long's conclusion about Huna is very similar to the opinion of Mikao Usui's view on Reiki healing.

Usui went on a quest to find the inner teachings of Jesus and was introduced to the Reiki healing symbols by way of a channeled vision. According to Long's reasoning, Reiki would simply be considered one of many versions of the ancient religion he would later name "Huna," which means "hidden secret" in Hawaiian. Long believed all esoteric teachings had the same beginnings and resulted in various philosophies of the same concept.

In 1945, Long founded the Huna Research Associates (HRA). In 1948, the HRA formed the Telepathic Mutual Healing Group to provide planetary healing based on Huna principles which will be discussed later in this book.

The HRA is now located in Cape Girardeau, Missouri, and continues to meet and hold conferences and discussion groups concerning Huna.

Long passed away in 1971. Thirty years after his death, Huna research continues through the HRA and many other teachers who have added their own interpretations of Long's work. After Long's death, the HRA was under the leadership of Otha Wingo and has recently passed on to his son, Vincent.

In California, where Long spent much of his time, another group formed a Huna *Heiau* Church, taking

Long's teachings a step beyond the original intent by actually creating a new quasi-religion out of Huna. Yet others have combined the science of Neuro-Linguistic Programming with Huna to create a further deviation from the original concept.

In recent years, Huna has become more prevalent in the United States. Today there are several thousand practitioners of Huna throughout the States who have taken Long's original work and added their own interpretations to it to create what we now call Huna.

The purpose of this book is to examine and dissect the original Huna as it was developed by its actual creator: Max Freedom Long.

Six

Key Concepts of Huna

It is important before going any further to discuss
and define several fundamental terms involved with
understanding Huna. I have included here a list of
terms which will be used throughout the rest of the
book. Please note, however, that this is a list of the
definitions of the terms according to Huna, the creation
of Max Freedom Long, and therefore may or may not
be accurate definitions of the words according to the
Hawaiian culture.

Remember that Long claimed to dissect Hawaiian
chants to draw conclusions of the meanings of many
concepts listed below. Also keep in mind, as mentioned earlier, the language is extremely complex and
difficult to translate due to its simplicity and lack of
many consonants and vowels.

In part two of the book, I will go over many of the
real Hawaiian meanings for the terms described below.

'Aumakua

According to Huna, the *'aumakua* is the higher self
of a person, the part of man that is connected to God
and knows all he or she has done as a soul in many
lifetimes. One of the primary principles of Huna is that

one cannot manifest anything on the physical plane without correctly learning to contact and communicate with the higher self. In his writings, Long spells the word "*aumakua*;" however, according to the *Hawaiian Dictionary*, the correct spelling has an apostrophe proceeding the word and it is that spelling we will use for the rest of the book.

Uhane

According to Huna, *uhane* is the conscious mind, or ego of the person, which resides in the solar plexus region of the body.

Unihipili

According to Huna, the *unihipili* is the unconscious mind of man, a childlike part of each person that must be trained and controlled so that it may learn how to communicate desires to the higher self. Long said that it is the unconscious mind that communicates with the higher self, not the conscious mind. Therefore, much of Huna discusses techniques to be used to train and build rapport with the unconscious mind.

Mana

Hawaiian term for "supernatural, divine power, or vital force." Also called *ki* in Japan, *chi* in China, *prana* or *kundalini* in India. It is electrical in nature, has magnetic qualities, and according to Long and the

HRA, is symbolized by water.

According to Huna, there were three types, or levels, of *mana*: *mana*, which was used by the *unihipili*, or unconscious mind is the lowest level; *mana-mana*, the willpower used by the ego and the conscious mind, or *uhane*; and *mana-loa*, used by the *'aumakua*, or higher self, the most powerful form of *mana*.

One may also note similarities of this word to the expression "manna" found in the Bible. In the Bible, manna is the term used to describe the "bread of life," as in the following passage:

"And he humbled thee, and suffered thee to hunger, and fed thee with manna, which thou knewest not, neither did thy fathers know; that he might make thee know that man doth not live by bread only, but by every word that proceedeth out of the mouth of the LORD doth man live." Deuteronomy 8:2-4

The exact definition of the biblical manna can be found in the *Dictionary of Religion*, which says: *"In the Hebrew Bible, the miraculous food provided to the Israelites during their wilderness wandering."*

Manna could also be described as the bread of life, or life force.

Ha (Breath)

Hawaiian term for "to breathe" and the number four. According to Long and the fundamentals of Huna, a technique used to raise the *mana* in the body to perform miracles and answer prayers.

The Christian missionaries who first came to the islands were observed to not use the breath while forming prayer and were referred to as "*ha'ole*" by the Hawaiians, which literally translates to "without breath." The term is still used today to describe non-Hawaiians.

It is interesting to note the striking similarity between this word and the word "holy" used in the Bible.

Thoughtform

In Huna, each thought we have occupies space and has it's own *aka*, meaning "shadowy body" in Hawaiian. The thoughts can "survive" and continue to take up space long after we think them. This is the same theory that permeates much of the current knowledge we now have of quantum physics. In Huna, Long concluded that related thoughts "stick" to each other and form clusters of thoughts. These thought clusters are sent to the high self during prayer by following specific procedures outlined in the practice of Huna which encompass the *ha* breathing techniques discussed earlier. In Huna, these thoughtforms can be either positive or negative and they can take on a life of their own to a certain degree, potentially wreaking havoc on their owner.

This concept is similar to that of spirit attachment mentioned in Reiki. Energy work can be used to alleviate unwanted thoughtforms in both disciplines.

Many modern authors including Deepak Chopra in the book *Quantum Healing*, and others have mentioned similar concepts. Chopra discusses the etheric double extensively and the fact that it is the representation of man in perfect form, in perfect health. The body regenerates itself every few years, yet because of energetic blockages and thoughtforms, it regenerates itself imperfectly.

In my opinion, it is the goal of energy work to facilitate the release of energy blockages that are hindering the person from tapping into the blueprint of his or her own perfection.

Aka

Hawaiian term for "shadow." In Huna, the *aka* body is the shadowy substance or ectoplasm that is a part of the spiritual man. Long said there is an *aka* cord that connects us to each other and to various objects. Anything we come in contact with attaches to us through our *aka* cords. *Aka* is an etheric substance used to channel or direct *mana* to the high self. It could also be another term for the etheric double of a person.

Long did much research on *aka* and its applications in various psychical sciences including telepathy, psychometry and mind reading.

Telepathy, according to Huna, occurs when we create thoughtforms, or thoughts, and then consciously transfer them to another person by sending them over our *aka* cord, which we mentally and psychically attach to the other person.

Mind reading, on the other hand, is when we send our *aka* substance out to another person, connect with them, and then allow ourselves to pick up their thoughtforms and bring them to us over our own shadowy *aka* cords so we can then see what a person is thinking.

Psychometry is done in much the same way, and Long wrote many books on this subject. All people, objects, and things have *aka* cords, therefore, psychometry can be performed by holding an object in the hands, and then following the *aka* cords to see where they go—perhaps to a place, or to a previous owner, or to a memory of an event.

In the book *Psychic Detectives*, by Colin Wilson, the author mentions Long's work and describes how this technique is used to find missing persons. The "psychic detective" does so by simply holding a personal item, and following the energetic cords back to the owner to pick up information on the individual's whereabouts.

Long also conducted much research into psychometric analysis after studying the work of Dr. Brunler and his famous Biometer.

The Biometer was originally invented by a man named Bovis and later fine-tuned by Dr. Oscar Brunler. The device was used to measure mental or brain radiations from people in an effort to determine the ability of the brain to combine intuitive abilities with logical reasoning functions. Brunler created a measurement scale used to obtain a numerical value to determine the true intelligence of a person. The measurement was called the Brunler Scale. Brunler conducted extensive research to analyze the brain power of various deceased individual geniuses from throughout history. Long became fascinated with the work and began incorporating it into the practice of Huna.

After much contemplation and study, Long and the other HRA's set out to study handwriting of many famous people including Joseph Stalin, Franklin D. Roosevelt and Madame Blavatsky, to name a few. Findings of their research can be found in Long's book, *Psychometric Analysis*. In this work, Long teaches the reader how to make his or her own biometric device and how, by using a pendulum, one can begin to analyze people's psyches using the readings given by the meter.

Long was also intrigued by the work of the late Verne L. Cameron, who invented the Cameron Aurameter, which replaces the pendulum in many instances and can be used for dowsing for water. Even 30 years after Cameron's death in 1970, his Aurameter continues to provide the most accurate readings available for dowsers.

Long applied many teachings of psychical science to the Huna philosophy, and seems to have continually added to the studies of various methods over the years the HRA was under his leadership.

The psychometry and psychometric analysis is, in my opinion, some of the most interesting work Long did. Of all the areas Long worked in, this one seems to have had the greatest impact on the work of other paranormal researchers. Many modern authors have been able to draw upon and expand on Long's work in this area. Many of these books are now out of print and available only by contacting the HRA in Missouri.

Ho'oponopono

The word *ho'oponopono* literally means "to correct error." It is the Hawaiian code of forgiveness. In some of his later work, Long created a powerful Huna process, which calls for the cutting of *aka* cords between people. Most modern Huna practitioners now use this process. Long said that since we have *aka* cords connected to every thing and everyone we have known, it is beneficial to go through a process of "error correction." Through *ho'oponopono*, we can forgive and be forgiven, make amends with everyone, then cut cords with them so we may release our *mana* to be used for our own needs.

Long believed that by freeing up our *mana* with cord cutting, we have more of it to put forth on our life's purpose.

Seven
Jesus and the Four Gospels

In the book *What Jesus Taught in Secret,* Long does a thorough, intensive study of some of the major tenets of the Bible and how they relate to Huna. He attempts to "prove" that Jesus was in fact a *kahuna* of the highest degree. Many examples in the book attempt to show that various biblical references were actually code words used in Huna.

One was the concept of turning water into wine (*John: 2:1-11*). Long interpreted this as Jesus taking his *mana* (symbolized by water in Huna) and turning it into wine, or an answered prayer by the higher self.

The reference to the Father, Son and Holy Ghost of the Bible are also compared in Long's translation of Huna. Long felt the father was the *'aumakua,* due to the literal translation of the word which means "utterly trustworthy parental spirit." The Son was the *uhane,* or conscious mind, and the Holy Ghost was the *unihipili,* or unconscious mind. The Holy Ghost, Long speculated, may also relate to the *aka,* or shadowy body. It was the "ghostly" unconscious mind that could send the telepathic message of prayer to the Father.

In Matthew, there is a reference to the planting of seeds which Long describes as the making of a prayer to present to the higher self for manifestation on the physical plane. In the following passage, the tree refers to the answered prayer:

> *"The kingdom of heaven is like to a grain of mustard seed, which a man took, and sowed in his field: Which in deed is the least of all seeds: but when it is grown, it is the greatest among herbs, and becometh a tree, so that the birds of the air come and lodge in the branches thereof."*
> *Matthew 13:31-32.*

Long also explains the manifestations of Christ as he appeared to his disciples following his death, passing through them as mentioned in Luke 4:30 by transmitting his *aka* body to achieve a full manifestation of himself through his ectoplasmic shadowy *aka* body:

> *"But he passing through the midst of them went his way."* *Luke 4:30.*

Long speculated that this, as well as the incident of Jesus walking on water recounted in all four Gospels, were both examples of how Jesus appeared in spirit via his *aka* body, or etheric double.

Long's books discuss his theories that throughout the four Gospels are several dozen references to various similarities of the Bible to Huna. He theorizes that Jesus had traveled extensively throughout Egypt and India learning the esoteric teachings and became a powerful healing *kahuna*. Jesus learned the secret code from the tribes of Egypt and the Bible was simply an attempt to preserve the teachings in the coded writings so that it could be used by future generations.

Long points out that throughout modern society

we have seen many religions take the Bible literally instead of attempting to look inside and underneath the spoken word to locate the symbols hidden there.

Long claimed that the Polynesian translation for the word "carpenter" happens to be "*kahuna*." This "proves," as far as Long was concerned, that Jesus was in fact a *kahuna*. Actually, this definition is false, which we will discuss later in the book.

There is no substantial evidence to support any of Long's theories regarding Jesus as *kahuna*, in my opinion; but it does make for some interesting (and often amusing) reading.

Eight
Principles of Huna – The Three Parts of Man

As mentioned earlier, according to the theories proposed by Long and the HRA, man had three parts: the conscious mind, *uhane*, unconscious mind or *unihipili*, and the superconscious, or *'aumakua*.

It is necessary to more fully consider these concepts now and how they interrelate to create the entire system of Huna, because it is the very foundation of the teachings.

It is interesting to note that others have interpreted the word *'aumakua* differently. For example, in the late Scott Cunningham's book *Hawaiian Magic and Spirituality*, the Hawaiians worshipped the *'aumakua* and they prayed to *'aumakua* who were ancestral spirits, or deceased relatives of the person. It was the *'aumakua* in both interpretations who would answer our prayers. The translation differences can easily be interpreted by the language complexity as well. After studying this topic extensively, I am inclined to lean toward Cunningham's definition as being closer to the actual interpretation, because it is backed up in the *Hawaiian Dictionary*, which defines *'aumakua* as "family or personal god." More information on this will follow in the second part of the book.

In Long's interpretation, there is only one way for a

prayer to be answered. That is through a process in which the conscious mind, *uhane*, makes a decision about what it is that is wanted or what the desired condition should be. *Uhane* communicates this to his *unihipili*, or unconscious mind, and then has *unihipili* send the message in the form of symbols telepathically up to the *'aumakua*. If the process is not carried out in this manner, the prayer cannot be heard.

But how can we work with our *unihipili* in the first place to make sure it understands what is to be done? Long discusses the fact that it must be trained. Just as a small child must go to preschool to learn proper behavior, the *unihipili* must be given similar treatment.

Long suggests giving it a name. He chose to call his *unihipili* "George." Many of the Huna Research Associates follow his example and do the same. By using a pendulum and a chart, one can train their "George" to follow directions and learn. Long said that by training "George" to answer simple "yes" and "no" questions he can be taught to eventually do the more complex work required to take prayer up to the *'aumakua*.

Developing a relationship with "George," according to Long, is like developing any relationship. You must get to know his likes and dislikes. You may feel compelled to ask him how he feels about certain subjects or people and get his response.

Building rapport with the unconscious mind is one of the keys to the psychometric analysis process mentioned earlier. Long felt one had to train "George" to respond to yes and no questions, and have strong rapport with him in order to be a competent psychometric analysis reader.

"George" can also learn to extend his *aka* shadowy

Three Parts of Man According to Huna

3 Selves	Translation	Spiritual Qualities	Functions	Deity	Mana
Aumakua	"Utterly Trustworthy Parental Spirit"	Superconscious, god/goddess within the individual, connects us to higher realms, perfection	Recognizes cause, can remove complexes, predicts future, realization - KNOWING	Kane	Mana-Loa
Uhane	"Rational mind" - persona	Conscious mind - what we think whether right or wrong, "free will" can "sin," has no memory	Decision maker and judge, "in charge" of unconscious mind, sorts and gathers information	Lono	Mana-Mana
Unihipili	"Low or Basic Self"	The real self, deep, emotional, illogical, telepathy, symbolic	Stores and represses memories, runs autonomic body functions, preserves the body, servant, follows orders, fight or flight	Ku	Mana

The physical body, symbolized by Kanaloa, is the vehicle for the three selves body through various activities. In the book *Secret Science at Work*, Long described exercises in which small objects were placed in boxes, and "George" was asked to pick a particular item out of the bunch by extending his *aka* body into the box and sensing where the desired object was located.

Of course, the most important reason to get to know your "George," according to Long, is for the successful delivery of prayer to the higher self. It is only through this process that one can achieve total fulfillment and enlightenment.

When forming prayer and deciding what it wants, the conscious mind, *uhane*, may get clarity from "George" that he understands the request and is ready to fulfill it. The *uhane* can only feel confident that this has actually occurred if he has trained "George" to respond to him.

A big part of this process involves raising the *mana*, or vital force, in the body by doing breathing exercises called the *ha* breath. Long felt that because breathing was one of "George's" major job duties, that when *uhane* chose to take that job over for him, it caught his attention so he would automatically know that something important was about to happen.

This also freed "George" up to now expend his efforts and energies in doing the work of delivering prayer.

In the *ha* breath, the person will breathe in through the nose, hold the breath for a few seconds, then breath out the mouth quickly while making a *ha* sound. Then another pause is required. It is in the times of pausing that the *mana* is actually beginning to flow through the body. After 10 sets of four breaths, the prayer is ready to be sent up to the *'aumakua*. One is to imagine that the *unihipili* is located in the solar plexus area and with each breath imagine an *aka* cord of energy going higher and higher until it connects to the energy flowing in through the top of the head, or crown chakra, which is the *'aumakua*. Then the prayer is read after the connection is made, and sent to *'aumakua* to allow the higher self to begin making the prayer manifest on the physical plane.

This is the fundamental process of Huna, and the most important part of the practice. The prayer must be repeated often, perhaps daily, and given energy if it is to become reality. The old adage: "Where attention goes, energy flows," comes to mind at this point.

Again, the premise behind this process is that the middle self does not have the capability to speak with the *'aumakua* directly. This is Long's explanation for why so many prayers go unanswered, particularly in the Christian religion.

Part 2

Discovering
the
Secret
of
Huna

Nine
Visit to the Islands

My initial frustration with this project from the beginning was the fact that no matter where I went to learn about Huna, I could never find any cultural Hawaiians to talk to me about it.

This was the first of many red flags that prompted me to write this book in the first place. My initial question was: "If this is the teaching of the *kahuna*, then can I please speak to someone or read a book from someone other than a *ha'ole* (Caucasian person)?"

Of course, no book on Huna would be complete without a thorough survey of Hawaii itself. Even those who teach Huna in the states now usually travel over to the islands for training programs.

My deceased counselor, Max Freedom Long, continued to channel thoughts and lessons to me and insisted I visit the islands for an extensive stay, particularly since it had been many years since my last visit to Hawaii.

I asked my guide what specific things I needed to prepare for, or contacts I needed to have and was assured I would find all I needed once I arrived.

The project was an exercise in stilling the mind and listening to my intuition which would take me and show me what I needed to know. Sure enough, that was exactly what happened. What I saw there was beyond my wildest expectations.

OAHU

I spent the first part of my stay in Honolulu exploring the city via the public bus system and visiting geographically significant sites such as the Diamondhead Crater.

Overlooking the magnificent Waikiki Beach, the Diamondhead Crater is one of the most visited tourist attractions in all of Hawaii. The crater got its name in the early 19th century when British settlers mistook the shiny calcite crystals found in the crater for diamonds. The site once served as a burial ground for the Hawaiian people.

My next stop would have to be to the place where Huna actually started: the Bishop Museum.

The Bishop Museum

Visit to the Islands

The Bishop Museum

The Bernice Pauahi Bishop Museum was built in 1889 by Charles Reed Bishop to honor his late wife, Princess Bernice. The Princess created quite a controversy by choosing to marry Bishop, a descendent of the missionaries, instead of Kamehameha V.

The original purpose of the museum was to house ancient Hawaiian artifacts and royal heirlooms, but it has since expanded into an incredible scientific museum and now houses an enormous collection of spectacular artwork from throughout the Polynesian islands.

This site is important to Huna because it is here that the entire story begins. The young Max Freedom Long claimed to have befriended the museum's first curator, William Tufts Brigham, and to have become his youthful protégé, heir to the initial research about Huna.

The staff at the Bishop is incredibly knowledgeable about all things Hawaiian, which was immediately evident.

At first, I spent some time at the museum looking carefully at the exhibits, and eventually found my way into the library.

In my initial visits, I was still unclear as to exactly what I was looking for or what questions I should be asking. I spent this time doing research on the actual customs of the *kahuna* and ancient Hawaiian spiritual matters. This information will be discussed in detail later.

The other thing I checked was to see if I might have made some mistake searching the Bishop's web database. Prior to my trip, I had put both "Huna" and "Max Freedom Long" into the Bishop's search engine and it turned up zero results, which I found to be peculiar. Surely they had information on Huna and Max Freedom Long there. I hoped I had been mistaken in assuming that it did not exist.

I was somewhat amazed, yet not completely shocked, to find that there was no mention of either Huna or Long at the museum. Some of the staff did not know about Huna at all, and those who did were quick to discount it. It was not a Hawaiian concept since it was, in fact, created by Long, and therefore did not have any place in the cultural archives of the Hawaiian people. It was as simple as that.

Island Hopping

The next part of my journey included extensive travel throughout each of the inhabitable islands—Maui, Hawaii, Molokai, Lanai and Kauai—before returning to Oahu, home of Pearl Harbor, the city of Honolulu, and the Bishop Museum.

The only places I did not travel were the islands of Kaho'olawe, which is currently covered by land mines which the state government is trying to clean up for future tourism possibilities, and Ni'ihau, a small island with few residents that is accessible by invitation only.

One common theme prevailed as I traveled around the islands photographing various sacred sites and speaking to the local people. I was always met with one of two responses regarding Huna: either they had never heard of it, or they thought it was a hoax.

I found myself trying to explain to the people that on the mainland there were *ha'oles* teaching classes to people so they could become "certified *kahuna*." The Hawaiian locals I spoke to could not believe their ears!

MAUI

I decided to go with the flow and allow myself to be completely led by my guide, Max. I bought an airline pass, which would allow me to travel freely throughout the islands, taking as many flights as I wanted whenever I wanted. That way, I would be free to go wherever the wind carried me.

My initial plan was to leave Oahu and head straight for Hawaii; however, as I arrived at the airport and went to the counter I found myself unexpectedly spitting out the word "Maui" when the ticket agent asked me where I would like to go.

The next thing I knew, I was on my way to Maui.

Iao Needle

One of my first stops was to what is probably the most famous spot on the entire island, the Iao Needle. Located in the Iao Valley, which literally means "Valley of Dawning Inspiration," or "Supreme Light," this is the site of the famous Battle of Kepaniwai (meaning "damning of the waters") where in 1790 King Kamehameha I fought and seized control of Maui in a bloody battle. At that time the river was a significant site to the Maui residents and was a main source for the island water supply. After the battle ended, the river ran red with blood and was clogged with hundreds of dead bodies from this bloody war.

In the late 1400s, much of this area was declared off-limits to visitors because it was known as the burial site for the *ali'i*, or Hawaiian royalty. Since that time the remains of many *ali'i* were found in this area.

Above:
The Iao Needle

Left: The Iao Valley
located east of the
Iao Needle, is the
famous site of the
Battle of Kepaniwai.

Visit to the Islands

Haleakala Crater and the Hana Highway

The next spot I feel compelled to describe is the Haleakala Crater National Park, which was the volcano that created the island of Maui. Tourists come from all over to witness the spectacular sunrises on top of the crater. Temperatures at the top are near freezing, even in summer, as the elevation is quite high.

The area looks like what we would think the surface of an uninhabited planet would be like. It is absolutely amazing.

Afterwards, I ventured down the East Coast of Maui on the famous Hana Highway despite warnings of an outbreak of Dengue Fever, which is a very serious illness carried by mosquito bites. I heard the warning, but decided not to allow that to stop my adventures. Nothing a good can of bug repellent couldn't stop, I figured.

I was certainly glad I went, as this is the most scenic and lush part of the island. The area is filled with lush jungles to hike in and stunning black lava beaches. The feeling here, particularly on the beach, is one of tremendous spiritual power and peace.

HAWAII

The next stop on the tour was the big island of Hawaii. I was anxious to visit this one again, as it had been many years since I had been there.

I stayed in Hilo, the rainiest city in the United States, located on the East Coast of the big island, just north of the Kilauea volcano.

When I first arrived, I unloaded my backpack and

Haleakala Crater National Park

The summit of Haleakala is 10,023 feet. This area is considered to be an active volcano, although the most recent volcanic activity on Maui occurred in 1790.

headed straight for the beach. It was there, not a half a mile away from my hotel, where one of the strangest experiences I have ever had occurred.

I was wading in the cold water of the sea when I happened to notice a huge wolf-like dog standing on top of an embankment. The beach was fairly crowded, yet for some reason, I knew the dog was looking right at me. I also knew he was headed my direction.

When I was about four years old, I was playing in my uncle's back yard when without warning, the family German Shepherd came up and attacked me. He had my head in his mouth and actually tore a piece of my nose off. I still have the scar of a toothmark in my temple and a new tip of my nose to prove it.

Shamanic tradition teaches that when you survive an attack from an animal, that the animal automatically becomes a totem for you. I have grown up particularly attracted to cats, which can also be explained because you may end up enjoying the company of animals who are enemies of your totem.

So on this particular day in Hilo, I was amazed with myself as I knew the huge animal was coming for me, yet I was not afraid. I decided to hold my ground and be calm. Sure enough, he came straight for me and began to stand on his hind legs and put his giant paws around me.

I was calm, but the people who were with me were scared to death. They tried to shoo the dog away by yelling and pointing sticks, but the dog would not back down. The dog became very angry when anyone attempted to come between us and that in turn made me afraid.

Neighbors were called from nearby houses and they could not get the dog away. My new friends from the hotel where I was staying said later that this was the strangest thing that they had ever seen. To me, it was almost surreal. The dog kept jumping up on me and I would as calmly as I could tell him "no" and put his paws down, but he would not stop. I turned to walk away and the molestation continued. The dog jumped on my back and scraped his huge paws down my legs. I was literally black and blue afterwards and my legs were bruised for the next week and a half. I could not see how hideous it was but would occasionally see people's faces as they were obviously staring at the back of my legs wondering what happened.

I spent some time wondering what the meaning was to all of this and what in me attracted such strange behavior.

Mo'okini Heiau and Kamehameha Birthsite

The next day I rented a car and headed north to the Mo'okini *Heiau* and the Kamehameha birthplace.

Mo'okini Heiau was used by Pa'ao and is one of few documented sites where human sacrifice actually occurred. Human sacrifice was rare in ancient Hawaii.

To get there I had to go down an unmarked dirt road in the middle of nowhere. There was literally not a soul in site as I began down to where the road came to a dead end.

I parked the car near the airport and headed down the road by the Upolu Airport, which is merely a paved airstrip. I hurried as fast as I could to get there as I had a full day ahead of me, yet it still seemed to take hours.

As I walked down the road, I was met by a baby bull that was blocking my path. He had apparently gotten out of the fenced in part of the pasture. I was afraid, especially after the dog incident the day before. I wished I had some of my crystals with me for strength.

I teach a gemstone healing class and use citrine as a power stone to activate strength and courage. I tried to keep my load light on this trip to the islands, however, so I left it at home. I stood on the road for a moment and meditated on the feeling of power and finally got my nerve up to walk past the bull. Nothing happened, which was a relief!

Then I visited the Mo'okini *Heiau* and was about to continue up the road to Kamehameha's birthsite when I was met by another domesticated wolf and a Doberman Pinscher. This really tested my strength. This time, I was all alone. There was no crowd on a beach to save me. I wanted to turn and forget it. After all, nobody would know if I did not complete the task—nobody but me, that is.

I got back into my power mediation, and proceeded to show no fear as I passed the growling animals. I walked with quick determination and felt a rush of relief as I passed them and looked down the road at the site I was so happy to see—the Kamehameha birthplace.

It was one of the largest *heiaus* I would see during my visit and was definitely worth the trouble.

I suppose it is hard to say for sure that this was the actual site of the birth itself, although scholars agree that the site is certainly near this area. Nevertheless the pristine condition of the large *heiau* combined with the incredible spiritual power of the site itself made it a worthwhile venture.

As I walked back to my car, I felt a sense of having completed some sort of test. I felt I had passed with flying colors and the confidence I had after that enabled me to walk with courage past the dogs again. This time, they did not growl but seemed to glance with respect as I walked by.

Then I once again encountered the baby bull. To my amazement, this time, as I approached he actually ran from me! He would stop for a moment and as I got closer, he would run again!

I had apparently completed some sort of rite of passage and the rest of my trip that day went perfectly.

Kamehameha birthsite from a distance.

MOLOKAI

Just like the trip to Maui, when I arrived at the airport thinking I wanted to head toward Kauai, I found myself asking for a seat to Molokai. This was one of the most fortuitous decisions I made during the entire trip. Of course, like I said in the beginning, I was not really in charge anyway. I was simply doing as I was told.

My first stop was to a site I had heard about and wanted to see for myself—the Phallic Rock.

Just as I had heard, this was definitely the most phallic rock I had ever seen. Just north of the airport a few miles, in the Palaau State Park was one of the most bizarre forests I have ever seen.

When I got there and parked my car, I was the only person around. I walked through the trees following the signs to the Phallic Rock. There were unusual pine-like trees everywhere with delicately thin, wispy, blue-green needles.

The forest had a strange energy to it and as I walked down the trail toward the rock, I found myself continually looking over my shoulder as if someone was watching me, yet I was completely alone, with the exception of the nature spirits. It was eerie and exhilarating at the same time.

The Phallic Rock

Within a half-mile walk, I came to the Phallic Rock. The legend is that there was a man who was caught admiring a beautiful young girl by the stream there when his wife caught him. In an argument, the man accidentally pushed his wife down a hill where she turned to stone. The man, who also turned to stone, is symbolized by the Phallic Rock. Supposedly, women can bring offerings and spend the night on the rock and return home pregnant. Because of this myth, the Park Service actually had to shut the place down for a time because activities there were getting out of hand.

A short walk from this site is an overlook where you can see down into the Wailau Valley, home of the world's highest sea cliffs and the former site of the leper colony tended to by the great priest Father Damien.

During the reign of King Kamehameha V, there was a terrible outbreak of leprosy on the islands and the ill were confined to this remote area to live the rest of their days under the care of Damien.

There is no mistaking the Phallic Rock!

LANAI

Lanai—also known as "the island of evil spirits" according to one local resident—was also an unexpected stop on the trip.

This is the island that Microsoft mogul Bill Gates rented out for his wedding a few years ago. According to locals, the resort where the nuptials took place is extremely haunted and all sorts of strange things happen there.

While I was in the airport in Molokai, I spoke with a local man who told me about a place called Sweetheart Rock on Lanai.

The legend said that there was a chief of Lanai in the old days who was married to a beautiful princess. He was extremely jealous and wanted to keep her all to himself, so whenever he had to go to battle, he would keep her out on top of a huge rock, isolated from other people. Once while he was away in battle, a great tidal wave crashed over the rock and killed the stranded princess. Her husband was so distraught over her death that he climbed the rock and threw himself into the ocean. The rock is now a sacred site with a *heiau* on top of it known as Sweetheart Rock. It is a very interesting site.

Another local resident I met in the airport told me to always be careful when photographing sacred sites and to ask the gods for permission. He told me a story about his aunt who had moved from the islands to the mainland and had come back to Hawaii for a visit. She apparently had forgotten the old ways and the respect for the land that one must adhere to. She had a video camera and was attempting to film a sacred site belonging to King Kamehameha I. Because she did not ask for permission, her film turned up blank.

Although I am happy to say none of my film turned up blank, I would later come to realize the value of his advice.

KAUAI

Finally, I was heading for Kauai for the last part of my tour of the islands. I was looking forward to spending quite a while here looking around, relaxing and enjoying all of the scenic beauty of the place. Once again, what I had planned was not at all what was actually in store for me.

Kauai is the oldest of all the islands, and therefore is teeming with *heiaus* and sacred sites of all sorts.

When I first arrived, I was so exhausted, I had to take a nap. When I awoke, my guide seemed to be pressing me to venture to the northern tip of the island to see the Kaulapaoa and Kaulaolaka *Heiaus*. I asked Max repeatedly if he was certain I could make it out

Sweetheart Rock off the shores of Lanai.

there by sundown, and he assured me I could. Traffic on Kauai is heavy, as there is only a two-lane road to get you around the island and often the two lanes cut down to one over bridges and narrow mountainous passes.

When I arrived at the parking lot near the sites, I figured I had about 45 minutes maximum until the sun went down. I hiked to the first site and saw many *kapu* signs guarding the site. *Kapu* means "taboo." The sign was in essence asking visitors to be respectful of the sacred areas and only walk up to them, keeping on marked paths, and not to cross over the walls.

I remembered what the man in Lanai said about being respectful of the sacred sites and humbly asked for permission to take photographs. I felt it was okay to do so and began to climb higher to get a closer look.

Unfortunately, I accidentally walked the wrong way down a path and found myself standing inside the forbidden area. I apologized and took a few photographs anyway; however, I felt I must have somehow offended the gods based on what happened to me the next day.

The next morning, I got up extra early to get a head start on visiting two other sites located on the North end of the island called Kipapa and Kapinao *Heiaus*. Their location was printed right on the tourist maps everyone gets when they arrive at the airport.

For some reason, though, I drove around and around and could never find them. I stopped for directions several times and could not believe how seemingly impossible it was to find this place.

I was about to give the whole thing up, assuming it was just not meant to be when I finally talked to someone who seemed to have actually been there himself.

He gave me the right directions, and soon I found myself parking the car and walking down the hill toward the first site.

I walked in the direction I thought was correct, camera in hand, ready to take some photos, when all of a sudden a blinding downpour of rain came down that caused me to begin slipping down the hill, nearly out of control.

I saw the site at last, and again remembered the words of the man in Lanai about knowing when it was not okay to take pictures. I respectfully put the camera away, knowing it was not a good idea, for one, and also realizing that the camera could get easily damaged by the torrential downpour.

As I slid down the hill to the foot of the site, all I wanted to do was get back up the hill to leave. I had a bad feeling I needed to go immediately. The problem was that the mud was getting so thick and running down the hill with such force, that I could not get a foothold to get out of there.

I began to panic a bit and found myself saying aloud, "Okay, I will be happy to leave, just let the rain stop so I can go!"

Almost as soon as I said the words, the rain slowed down and I was able to scramble up the hill, covered in mud and soaking wet from head to toe.

As soon as I reached the lot where my car was, the rain came to a stop and as I looked around I saw the surrounding area was dry and the clouds seemed to only be over the area where I was parked.

Was there a force there that did not want me around? Perhaps I was just paranoid. After all, Kauai is the Garden Isle with more average rainfall than the other islands; however, I still felt I was unwelcome there.

I struggled getting into the car without turning it into a muddy mess, and after getting myself situated, began to head south down the highway toward the other end of the island.

I decided it might be best to begin at the Napali Coast on the west side of the island and work my way back.

I planned to be in Kauai several days and considered spending the night in the national forest at Koke'e State Park, located in Waimea Canyon.

First, I thought I could explore another site called Polihale *Heiau* located on the Napali Coast. The drive was slow due to traffic and when I finally arrived I assumed again it would be easy to find. This time, it was. I asked for permission to photograph the site and felt it was okay.

Stone wall of the Kaulaolaka Heiau.

Right after I took a few photos, I suddenly began to have an eerie feeling of trepidation and heard my guide tell me I needed to get out of there and leave on the next flight back to Oahu.

It was already 1:45 p.m. and my rental car would have to be returned by 3:00 p.m. in order to avoid being charged for an extra day. I argued vehemently with my deceased friend that there would be no possible way for me to make this deadline with traffic as bad as it was.

He seemed to insist I leave at once, and arguing seemed to be of no avail. I got in the car and headed back toward the other side of the island.
As I passed the road to Waimea Canyon I felt a temptation to go ahead and drive up into the mountains to the state park, yet again felt the feeling of trepidation and instead drove on.

I decided I had to get at least one more photo to make my stop worthwhile, so I visited the sacred site of Fort Elizabeth, located in South Kauai.

It was here that a Russian Fort was built over an ancient *heiau*. It was an extremely interesting place, from a historical perspective. While I was walking the grounds there, I again felt the urge to call off my trip to Oahu and just stay longer—at least one more day.

Just as the thought entered my head, I was walking down the trail at Fort Elizabeth when I was suddenly stricken with a sharp, stabbing pain that caused my leg to almost collapse under me.

This happened twice before I finally made the final decision not to fight the gods anymore and just get out. As soon as I agreed to leave the pain subsided.

As I drove toward the rental car agency, I was reminded of when I was a young girl and went to Hawaii with my parents. We stayed on the islands of

Hawaii and Kauai, and I remembered that while on
Kauai, my dad was ill the entire time with a strange
virus and was so sick he could hardly walk or get out of
bed. It was certainly a strange "coincidence."

Traffic was horrible and I was hoping that if I had
to go I could at least be spared the extra expense of
having to pay for another day of the car.

Unbelievably, I arrived at the rental agency at 2:55
p.m. Five minutes to spare! I could not believe it!

The stunning Napali Coast.

I went to the airport ticket counter, expecting at least an hour layover. Instead I was told a flight was boarding in five minutes and I was just in time to make it. Signs all pointed to the fact that the island-hopping portion of my trip had come to an abrupt end.

Were the gods indeed cursing me for my accidental and ignorant disrespect? I have no idea. All I do know is that I was certainly relieved beyond belief when the plane left the tarmac, knowing I was about to begin phase two of my adventure.

Ten
Back to Oahu

When I finally arrived back in Oahu for the con-
tinuation of my research, Max led me to meet people
who, one by one, would lead me to more clues about
Huna.

I decided to call the University of Hawaii first and
speak to the chairperson of the Hawaiian Studies
Department, Lillikala Kame'eleihiwa, who basically
told me that Huna is a sore spot for many cultural
Hawaiians.

Prior to the late 20th century, as mentioned earlier,
all Native American religions were illegal to practice in
the United States. Therefore, particularly around the
turn of the century, nobody was going to discuss the
native religion to anyone publicly, especially a *ha'ole*
from California.

In all of Long's work, he assumes that the Hawaiian
people are totally ignorant of their heritage simply
because they did not tell him about it. This is not the
case at all. The secrets did not go to the graves; people
were taught at a very young age to never speak about
their religion to anyone at all outside the family. To do
so would often mean fines and/or imprisonment.

Kame'eleihiwa stated that to this day, the Hawaiian
people do not want to share many of the local prac-

tices, as is the case with many mainland native customs. Certainly there are some things we can know, but not everything. Publishing such items would, in essence, disempower the family.

The problem that these laws have caused for the Hawaiian culture is the fact that many young people are now growing up believing that Huna is their heritage simply because there were so few books published prior to 1990 on their real cultural heritage. There were some fabulous books, such as Beckwith's Hawaiian Mythology, King David Kalakaua's *The Legends & Myths of Hawaii*, as well as other books from great writers such as Malo and Komakau, all of which are extremely scholarly in nature and may not appeal to the lay person. In addition, by sheer volume, there were not as many of these type books prior to 1990 as there were books written on the subject of Huna, which is also a subject easily accessible through numerous websites. It is easy to see how this error could be made based simply on the number of publications available to the public about Huna.

The mission to educate people about the true cultural heritage is one on which the Hawaiian people are working diligently through publications, classes and lectures, all of which have become more prevalent in recent years.

I noticed there seemed to be more emphasis on educating tourists on the spiritual nature of the Hula, and there are new tourist attractions, such as the Polynesian Cultural Center on Oahu, which has displays and educational programming to teach the Polynesian culture to visitors.

Although Huna is a problem for the people of Hawaii and measures are being taken to educate the public, there are more pressing issues facing the Hawaiian people at this time. Therefore, discrediting Huna does not take a top billing on the list of priorities.

One of the places dedicated to educating the public is the local publisher and bookstore called Native Books.

It was suggested I visit Native Books to acquire some of the real Hawaiian spirituality books. As "luck" would have it, when I visited and told the people about my work, the owner came out to meet me personally and offered to call local author, Pali Lee. Lee co-authored two books on Hawaiian spirituality with her late husband, John Koko Willis.

I called Lee and was pleased that she invited me to her home to discuss Huna. What Lee told me during our two-and-a-half-hour conversation changed the course of my entire work. It was then that I had finally received the information I needed to begin asking the right questions.

Eleven
The Secret Revealed

At the time I called Lee to make the appointment, she told me something I had never imagined: that Max Freedom Long had committed suicide because he was guilty about all of the lies he told.

My mouth fell open in disbelief. Was this woman crazy, or was there some validity to her story?

What motive could she possibly have to make up such a thing and did she have any proof of her theory?

Before our meeting, I was determined to look into her claims to see if any of what she said could be substantiated.

She told me about some letters Max Freedom Long wrote to a man named Theodore Kelsey, and claimed that these would hold some significant answers to my questions.

I realized I had some serious work to do before our meeting.

Theodore Kelsey

Theodore Kelsey was born in Seattle, WA, in 1891 and arrived in Honolulu with his family in 1895. At an early age, he began to teach himself the Hawaiian language and became instrumental in the research done to translate and record the ancient Hawaiian chants. His contributions to the Hawaiian culture are priceless and have played a key role in the preservation of ancient customs.

From 1936-1939 Kelsey worked in the Hawaii State Archives and it was during this time that Long corresponded with him.

Because Long based his Huna theories on the fact that he had translated ancient Hawaiian chants to discover the secrets of the *kahuna*, it is not surprising that he chose to contact Kelsey in regards to his book. Kelsey was, after all, one of the foremost authorities on ancient chants in all of Hawaii.

According to Lee, the letters Long wrote to Kelsey were stored in the Hawaii State Archives, should I choose to look them up. They supposedly referred to the original manuscript of the book *Recovering the Ancient Magic*, which was the precursor to *The Secret Science Behind Miracles*.

This was an interesting story. Long claimed to have consolidated his research of the inner workings of Hawaiian *kahuna* to the point that he had no more information to share, and at that point began to search for a publisher. He wound up getting the book published in England. The night before the book was to be sent out into the hands of the public, a bomb blew up the building and all of the copies and plates were destroyed and had to be totally redone. The book from then on remained relatively obscure and even now it is only available through the Huna Research Associates in Missouri.

Was the universe trying to tell Long something by blowing his work to bits? We can only speculate.

I went to the Hawaii State Archives and looked up Kelsey's personal correspondence. Sure enough, there was a file called Max Freedom Long.

In the file there are letters between the two which suggest that Long had indeed sent his manuscript to Kelsey to get his opinion of the work.

In a letter dated March 25, 1936, Kelsey wrote Long the following letter after receiving his book:

"Dear Mr. Long:

Thank you very much for the fine book you wrote, and sent me, also for the box of valuable material.

I am going over the material with my special teacher and good friend Professor Fred Beckley, former professor of the Hawaiian Language at the University of Hawaii, who holds the honorary degree of Doctor of Hawaiian Literature, from Oxford College, England....

I am sorry to say that Prof. Beckley has an exceedingly poor opinion of Dr. Brigham, whom you have made the 'hero' of the book, as it were. He was no linguist in Hawaiian, as you think. His twenty-two years at the Museum were practically wasted as far as preserving anything Hawaiian were concerned. Dr. Gregory, his successor, found a mass of untruth, and little done. He also considers that the character of Dr. Brigham had a grave flaw. Personally, I consider a man's ability and attainment, overlooking personal defects. But then one has to consider before making a man a 'hero' of a book."

In the rest of the letter, Kelsey transcribes the notes of Professor Beckley and shows the correct definitions of many of the terms used in Long's manuscript, basically telling Long that his entire translation is completely erroneous.

In a letter dated August 28, 1940, Long wrote to Kelsey in regard to the fact that Kelsey had taken his manuscript to another man to look at. Long seemed appreciative and had the following to say:

"Dear Mr. Kelsey:

You were a brick to take the MMS to Mr. Belasco and to tell me about him as you did in your letter which has just come in the last mail...

It is my hope that he may hunt around and find kahunas *of sorts eventually, even to the point of getting one of them to check again the theories I have evolved and propounded in the MMS and by letter covering the matter of the astral body and* kino aka. *It would be nice to know one way or another whether I am near the mark or barking up the wrong tree, as our good friend Prof. Beckley thinks...*

One reason I cling so to my ideas is that they almost parallel ideas held by my English friend, W. R. Stewart, who took the kahuna *training in part from the Berbers in North Africa. These Berbers do not speak anything like Hawaiian, but still have Polynesian words to describe their* kahunas *and* kahuna *beliefs...*

I am glad you have work of sorts. I had two months work recently sanding boards, but none since. I have been driving to get out a third murder book, borrowing money to live on as I did so, and between jumps have tried three pulp stories, on none of which I have yet had replies from magazines to which they were sent. There is one new pulp called "UNKNOWN" which handles yarns of magic and such things as if all were true and possible. Rather amusing reading. I sent two

*to it, both dealing with poltergeists and raids of ghosts
bent on obsessional activities. Too bad to have to try
such methods to get beans, but my own use of* kahuna
*magic is pretty fruitless these days. I must confess that
I don't try. Perhaps if I did I could get some results. It
is so hard to keep from slipping back into old habits of
thought and forgetting that I have decided with logic
that there are forces to be used and methods of using
them. We should all have a sixth or psychic sense to
help impress us that there are things which exist even if
we cannot see and eat them, what?*

*Again, my most sincere thanks for all your past and
recent assistance. I appreciate it all greatly.*

Sincerely, Max F. Long

In summary, it seems Long was advised that much
of his material contained incorrect information, but
was stubborn and held to his ideas simply to make
money.

In another letter to Kelsey, Long says that:

*"If my ambition is realized to develop an experi-
mental group out of my first little class beginnings, it
might well be that later on such translations of the old
healing prayers would be needed to practice with.
There are so many possibilities it seems one can do
almost nothing without some money to use, the latter
being always hard to come by to meet overdue taxes
and debts. However, things have brightened slightly
with our house at Laguna. A story sold for Louise and
Ethyl and there was the advance money on a third
detective novel—the first sales in over a year, so we got
almost a jump ahead of the wolf, what with my continual odd job work. If luck should hold and the novel*

*sell for a serial, then I could swing the printing of a
booklet on the* kahunas—*a thing I long to do as I feel
the information I have on the subject for Hawaiian and
Berber-Egyptian sources by now should be more
widely known in the interests of both science and
religion.*

*My class is very odd. Only two of the twelve have
any knowledge of psychology or psychic science, and
only two have any slight psychic ability. I am starting
to educate them from scratch, and their interest in the
beginning was mainly curiosity as to what I might have
to tell them. I am getting needed practice in working
with a group, which is good. Later on I hope that I
may get publications out and be invited to do more
lecturing and instruct in larger groups in cities where
the members would be able to donate enough to fi-
nance the work. It is all in the laps of the gods and
only time will tell what comes of it."*

Charles Kenn

In the correspondence between Kelsey and Long,
Kelsey mentioned that he passed Long's work on to a
man named Charles Kenn, who became a follower and
friend to Long.

Kenn apparently joined the Huna Research Associates for a time and wrote a small book on firewalking
rituals called *Firewalking from the Inside.*

In the Bishop Museum Archives there is a recorded
speech given by Charles Kenn in 1982 . Kenn was
apparently giving a lecture in the Bishop Museum
conference room, and during the question-and-answer
period someone asked about Max Freedom Long.

Kenn proceeded with some very interesting accusations:

"...I don't think he (Max) ever thought it (Huna) would become such a big deal. He wrote a few books about something no one seemed to know about and he could make a few bucks. California was a long way away in those days. He wasn't a prophet...I did say to him one time in the '60s, you have to be aware...what you send out is going to come back. It has to be more than what gets you through the night. We have a responsibility to others.

"...Max wrote in his book that he went to William Tufts Brigham at the Bishop Museum and Dr. Brigham told him "Where have you been? I have been looking for you for 49 years," and Dr. Brigham laid out to him on a silver platter, so to speak (all that he) knew about the kahuna. But the fact is, Brigham was no longer there. He was retired and was gone from Hawaii in 1921 when Max said he saw him. There were three men at the museum in 1921: John Stokes, the acting director, Kilolani Mitchell and Dr. Bryan. They all stated they never met Max Long...After I came back to Hollywood in 1949...(Max) was surprised that I investigated many of these things. I told him that he was not presenting the truth by saying he got his material from Dr. Brigham because Dr. Brigham never met him. I did not do it in an abrupt way, but I told him I had to withdraw his study."

This information was a true shocker. Certainly Kenn was entitled to his opinion about Long and his ethics, yet the accusations he made were amazing to me. Could it be that Long never actually met Brigham and made the whole thing up?

Unfortunately, Kenn is no longer alive to speak to personally. He passed away several years ago in Honolulu after being declared a "Living Hawaiian Treasure" by the Hawaii State Legislature.

It was disressing enough to see the Hawaiian scholar's discouraging words concerning Long's work and the errors it contained, but to think Long may have manufactured the meetings with Brigham was something else entirely.

I set out now to see if this statement by Kenn had any validity. The only way I could find out is by going to the source: the Bishop Museum.

Unfortunately, because we are dealing with a subject over 30 years old since Long died in 1971, many of the players in this drama, such as Kenn, are now deceased, and therefore, cannot be interviewed directly, unless they too could be channeled.

The most likely way to determine if this accusation is true is to thoroughly study Brigham himself.

William Tufts Brigham

William Tufts Brigham was born in Boston, Massachusetts on May 24, 1841. He graduated from Harvard in 1862 and came to Hawaii in 1864 for a two-year botanical exploration of Hawaii, before returning to Massachusetts where he taught botany at Harvard until 1869.

Brigham returned to Hawaii n 1887 and befriended Charles Reed Bishop, who was in the process of collecting historic cultural artifacts belonging to his late wife so that he could house them in the building that would later become the Bishop Museum.

Brigham was later appointed the first curator and later the first director of the museum where he was known to some as the greatest scientist in the history of Hawaii.

On a personal note, there are numerous accounts stating that the man hated people, particularly women, and surrounded himself by an all-male staff.

There are countless articles on Brigham in the *Honolulu Advertiser*, and other periodicals of the time, that all suggest the fact that although he was a genius in areas of science, this man was not at all friendly. He even went to the extreme of calling Queen Liliuokalani, Hawaii's last reigning monarch, a "squaw," and insulted the famed Father Damien by calling him a "rascal,"—an act that so insulted the Hawaiian people it nearly led to his dismissal as Director. The Hawaiian people see Damien as a national hero with near sainthood status.

After reading these articles, the descriptions of Brigham I had an opportunity to look at made me question the validity of Long's claims in the book *The Secret Science Behind Miracles*, particularly when Long describes his relationship with Brigham:

"At times he would open his heart to me. He was a great soul, and still simple." The Secret Science Behind Miracles, p. 13.

I now find this claim to be a bit preposterous after reading headlines about the man such as "Bishop's first director wasn't exactly 'Mr. Popularity,'" from an article in the *Honolulu Advertiser*, and seeing him refered to as: "a professional misanthrope." Having

Photo courtesy Bishop Museum

William Tufts Brigham, Director of the Bernice P. Bishop Museum, Honolulu, Hawaii, October 3, 1910.

heart did not seem to be one of Brigham's strong points at all.

And the sensational fashion in which Long claims Brigham chose him to be his protégé is also a bit melodramatic, by second glance:

"...in that hour he (Brigham) placed his finger on me, claiming me as his own, and like Elijah of old, preparing to cast his mantle across my shoulders before he took his departure. He told me that he had long watched for a young man to train in the scientific approach and to whom he could entrust the knowledge he had gained in the field—the new and unexplored field of magic." The Secret Science Behind Miracles, p. 12.

According to Director's reports from the Bishop Museum, Brigham retired from the museum in early 1918, and took a one-year leave of absence. He then returned in 1919 as Director Emeritus and Curator of Anthropology, where he began preparation of a memoir in Hawaiian worship.

In 1920, Brigham continued his travels by visiting Australia, and in 1921 he completed the work on Hawaiian worship.

Other than brief, one-or two-line descriptions of his work, there is no other mention of Brigham in the reports until the year of his death, 1926, which suggests he was not at the museum much during these years.

In fact, as early as 1920, there are letters and reports Brigham made to the new director and staff suggesting that his work was hampered by lack of suitable office space so he was forced to do what little he could at home. Sources say he was rarely in his office.

In the report of the Anthopology Department for 1920 Brigham says his wok was *"greatly hindered by my severance from the museum library and the photographic rooms."*

In addition, there are hundreds of documents stored in the archives relating to Brigham's life, including insignificant items such as grocery lists, appointments, and other miscellaneous notes. After personally looking through all of it, I did not find one single mention of Max Freedom Long anywhere.

If Long was as important to Brigham as he claims to be, would there not be some mention of him in Brigham's notes? One would think so.

In looking at Brigham's obituary, I stumbled across an article concerning his last will and testament. After reading the will in its entirety, I discovered that Brigham left all of his manuscripts to his sister and he requested his books be sold, then donated by the purchaser to the Punahou School in Honolulu. Again, if Long was indeed the man Brigham had been searching for all his life, would he not have been named in the will as a recipient of the manuscripts, or at least of some of Brigham's enormous book collection? Yet this is not the case at all.

In addition, after looking into some of Kenn's other comments, I checked the files for John Stokes, who assumed the role of curator in charge in 1919, after Brigham's retirement, as well as files for the new appointed director, Herbert Gregory, who served as director from 1920-1936. There was no mention of a Max Freedom Long anywhere, although several appointments and visitors were documented.

I find it unlikely that Long ever met Brigham.

Twelve
How Long Made Up Huna

If we may now assume that Long never met William Tufts Brigham, how did he go about constructing the fictitious conversations between the two and where did he get the information Brigham supposedly told him? Did he make the whole thing up, or was it loosely based on information he had uncovered?

Bishop Museum staff reports referred to a manuscript Brigham was working on prior to his death on Hawaiian worship. This document now exists only in the Bishop Museum Archives and has never before been published.

I was able to read the document while doing this research and discovered two parts that were of particular interest to me: one on firewalking, and the other on the death prayer.

The Firewalk

In *The Secret Science Behind Miracles*, Long claims Brigham told him of his adventures with *kahuna* friends who took him to an active volcano in South Kona, where they engaged in a sacred firewalking ritual. Long recounts the story as he claims Brigham told it to him.

Apparently the *kahuna* performed some kind of magic and put themselves into a trance after tying *ki* (pronounced "ti" - an indigenous sacred plant used in healing) leaves on their feet, and walked across hot lava with no damage to their feet. Brigham also apparently said that he did the same with his boots on and burned the soles from them but sustained no physical injuries after walking across the coals.

Long said that much to Brigham's surprise, his feet were uninjured, and he attributed his success to the sacred prayer ritual performed by his companions prior to his walk across the coals.

Ki leaves near a sacred site in Kauai.

According to Long's account, Brigham considered himself to be a total skeptic at the time he witnessed the event, and could not believe this was possible even after experiencing it for himself. Long said that Brigham later reached out to touch the coals with his hand, and was promptly burned. Certain that there was no scientific explanation for this phenomenon, Long said Brigham became convinced this was some sort of magic. The only problem was that Brigham could not figure out the secret that enabled the magic to happen. Long claimed that is where he came in, to finally help the old scientist, Brigham, discover how the magic really worked, and to carry on his "work" after his death.

It is interesting to note that in his unpublished manuscript, Brigham tells stories about firewalking practices of Tahiti and Fiji, which he read about in various reports on psychical research.

To satisfy his curiosity about the phenomenon he had only read about, Brigham decided to take a trip to Tahiti in 1901. While he was there, Brigham reported that he witnessed a priest named Papa Ita walk across hot basalt stones in a pit dug out especially for the purpose of engaging in a sacred firewalk. Papa Ita spoke with Brigham via a translator and told him he used a form of magic to enable him to easily walk across the stones with no injuries.

Brigham then makes a feeble attempt to draw a personal comparison between the phenomenon he saw in Tahiti, and a trip he took to Kilauea in which he walked a short distance *alone* over some hot lava and scalded his boots.

Here is a passage taken from Brigham's manuscript where he describes in his own words how he ventured over the hot lava—*alone*:

> *"No one was with me to remonstrate, and I de-*
> *cided to attempt to cross the recently cooled crust*
> *although the edges were still incandescent and lazily*
> *spluttering with a slight rise and fall of level...I made a*
> *great leap over the magic ring and there was a sensa-*
> *tion of sinking footsteps but I did not wait to examine*
> *any footprints...My shoes held together until I climbed*
> *the steep rail to the house, but were of no further use;*
> *my feet were not burned, but not more than when*
> *rowing in a hot sun for the same time and my hands*
> *were protected by buckskin gloves. I must have trav-*
> *eled many times the distance of the ordinary fire-*
> *walkers, but not barefooted although probably on*
> *hotter lava." Brigham MS*

In this account given by Brigham himself, he clearly says he went alone on this journey across the hot lava, unlike Long's account in which he is accompanied by some *kahuna* who watch him cross the lava in his boots.

I have spoken to many authorities on Hawaiian culture who have confirmed that there is no such thing as a firewalking ritual in Hawaii. It is primarily a tradition conducted in Fiji and Tahiti.

The only evidence I could find that this even existed at all was in a small, out-of-print book written in 1949 by Charles Kenn mentioned earlier called *Firewalking from the Inside*. In this report, Kenn describes inviting a chief from Huahine in the Society Islands to Honolulu to participate in a traditional Polynesian firewalking ceremony.

The group made a fire pit with basaltic stones and

conducted the experiment with the Huna Research Associates. The foreword of the book is written by Long, who applauds Kenn on his organization of the event, although he did not attend it, as there were no pictures of him or mentions of him anywhere else in the book.

In Kenn's book there is clearly no mention of any native Hawaiians participating in the study at all, although interim curator of the Bishop Museum John Stokes was there with his wife. This further validates Kenn's claim that Long never met the staff of the Bishop, including Stokes, because even at that event, Long was not in attendance.

The only other reference I could find to anyone who may engage in such firewalking ceremonies in Hawaii is a group called the Edith Kanakaole Foundation who worship the goddess Pele and may participate in a similar ceremony in honor of the goddess.

Some modern Huna practitioners participate in firewalking ceremonies by creating pits similar to the one Kenn described in his book.

This ritual also exists among members of the general population who participate in Anthony Robbins' seminars, often held in Hawaii, where students are asked to walk across hot coals after going into altered states of consciousness. Again, this custom is not, however, a native Hawaiian practice.

It is my opinion that Long read Brigham's unpublished manuscript and combined the information from Brigham's experiences with the Tahitian people and his walk to Kilauea to construct the story Long attributes to Brigham himself.

I base this conclusion on the similarity between the story told in the manuscript and the one told in Long's book, and the fact that I have questioned numerous native

Hawaiians about this topic and most tell me there is no such thing as the firewalk.

Death Prayer

The story of Brigham and the death prayer is also questionable. In the book *The Secret Science Behind Miracles*, Long described the story that Dr. Brigham apparently told him about an exploratory trip he took with a group of Hawaiians in order to collect plant specimens for study.

According to what Long said Brigham told him, an angered *kahuna* would find a person near death and charm his spirit out of his body to go and inhabit the body of a healthy person who was the target of the *kahuna's* vengeance. Long said the victim would receive the ill spirit and soon become sick and die. Contrary to what some non-Hawaiians would like to believe, this was a relatively uncommon occurrence.

In the story Brigham supposedly told Long, one young boy on the botany expedition suddenly became very ill with paralysis in his legs that seemed to slowly creep up his body.

Long said Brigham and the others in the group quickly recognized the symptoms to be those of a death prayer, and began to question the boy about who sent it.

Brigham supposedly told Long that the young man recalled a warning from his village *kahuna* saying that anyone who dared help the white man would receive the prayer of death.

Long explained that usually when a death prayer was sent, the *kahuna* would take action to shield and protect him or herself against a counterattack. In this case, according to Long, the sending *kahuna* did not take that precaution because he assumed the white people would not be able to retaliate.

Long said because Brigham was a scholar of Hawaiian lore, he attempted to send the prayer back to the *kahuna* who sent it by "rationalizing" with the spirit as to why this innocent boy should be saved. Brigham supposedly did this by making the discarnate entity understand that it was the *kahuna* who instead deserved to die. Long said Brigham told him how he made a lengthy and compelling argument in favor of his young companion.

Soon after Brigham made his plea, Long said the boy began to get better and made a total miraculous recovery.

The next day Long said Brigham and the scientific team took the boy home to his village and were curious to see what, if anything, had happened to the *kahuna*.

Sure enough, according to Long, the *kahuna* had died the night before, supposedly thanks to Brigham's success with the death prayer, and all who lived in the village feared and respected Brigham from then on.

I found it curious after reading Brigham's unpublished manuscript that he does indeed include a very brief section about the death prayer, and calls it by its proper name, *'ana-'ana*. In the true Hawaiian culture, there was such a person called a *kahuna 'ana-'ana* who had the ability to pray a person to death.

In Brigham's unpublished manuscript, he describes what he believes this process to be, and offers an example of an actual prayer he claims can be used to pray someone to death.

The document Brigham authored also contains a fascinating photo of an assumed *kahuna*, on his knees while in the middle of praying someone to death. I find that hard to believe because I do not think such a *kahuna* would allow himself to be photographed while engaging in that type of activity. The photo may merely represent what it could look like if we were to see it.

The main point I want to make here is that in Brigham's manuscript there is absolutely no mention of the botanical exploration Long described in *The Secret Science Behind Miracles*. There is no place in Brigham's unpublished manuscript that describes any activities such as those in Long's book about Brigham praying someone to death, or about a young boy being stricken with illness, or anything of the sort. In fact, unlike the firewalking situation where Brigham attempts to add a personal experience, he does not add any personal stories of any kind while discussing *'ana-'ana*. The section is very short and primarily contains the prayer itself.

I am not the first person to question Long about this. In a review of *The Secret Science Behind Miracles* recorded in 1953 at the Bishop Museum, Dr. Albert W. Palmer had this to say about Long's account of the death prayer:

"And when it comes to Dr. Brigham implying that he prayed an old Hawaiian kahuna *to death by use of* ana-ana *in reverse, I am sure Long must have dressed up that event in such a way Dr. Brigham himself would want to repudiate. If allowed to stand factually true it would seem to make Dr. Brigham guilty of manslaughter!"*

Palmer also pointed out in his review that much of the information in *The Secret Science Behind Miracles* is unsubstantiated due to the fact that Brigham was dead prior to the book's publication, and therefore could not authenticate the quotations.

Palmer knew Dr. Brigham personally and said Long's

entire portrayal of the man was inaccurate because of the dry, humorless, and overly sentimental manner in which he was depicted.

He also raised many of the same points that appeared in Charles Kenn's discussion: that Long may have indeed taken advantage of the fact that there was very little information written on Hawaii at that time, and that it would be difficult to debunk or discredit his work.

The Hawaiian culture was a topic few people wrote about, particularly on the mainland; theoretically, someone could say whatever he wished about the subject and there would be nobody around to refute it.

What is especially interesting is the fact that even now, more than 50 years later, much of Long's material is difficult to fully discredit due to the fact that there is still little published information on the true Hawaiian spiritual practices. Although it is getting easier for us to now know some of the customs of the Hawaiian people, the deep mysteries are still that: mystery.

One of the most intriguing and telling pieces of evidence concerning Brigham's lost manuscript is written right in the pages of *The Secret Science Behind Miracles* at the end of the first chapter:

"My own studies and those of Dr. Brigham are almost unknown in the Islands, and copies of my first report are kept carefully locked away in the library in Honolulu, being brought out only if requested by one who knows that it is there." The Secret Science Behind Miracles, p. 27.

Right there, this former mystery writer gives away the clue to the whole puzzle. The fact is, there is no document having anything to do with Max Freedom Long anywhere in Honolulu other than copies of his books at the state library.

I am certain the hidden document Long refers to containing the work of "Dr. Brigham and himself" has to be Brigham's unpublished manuscript housed in the Bishop Museum archives, and yes, is available only if you know it is there.

In *The Secret Science Behind Miracles*, Long claims this information is under such lock and key because the locals fear it and because of what it discusses concerning the death prayer. That is ridiculous. Long is merely an extremely creative writer.

Now for a closer look at the construction of the system of Huna itself and the terms Long created.

'Aumakua

In Long's world, the *'aumakua* was the higher self, the part of you and me that is connected to God and the life force, and the part that— if we follow his complex methods—we can communicate to so our prayers will be answered.

Long based this conclusion on the way he interpreted this word in the dictionary, plus the fact that I am sure he encountered it in many chants.

Long's interpretation of this is somewhat justified; however, in the context of the true Hawaiian culture it is incorrect.

What is the meaning of the word *'aumakua* according to the Hawaiian people? The *'aumakua* are deified ancestral spirits of the Hawaiian people—the collective spirit of the deceased ancestors of the people. The Hawaiian people worshipped their ancestors and turned to them for spiritual guidance.

According to Professor Beckley's remarks found in Theodore Kelsey's letter to Max Freedom Long:

"With regard to the " 'aumakua," Prof. Beckley feels that there were a pure original, and later contaminated conception. The original " 'aumakua" was a guardian angel that had not been incarnated, and was called " 'aumakua o ke ao." The later 'aumakua was the " 'aumakua o ka po." It is the Professor's theory that Pa'ao was an escaped Catholic priest who had made his way from Europe into the Pacific due to persecution of the Catholics following the Inquisition, and that his original name may have been Pavao. This Pa'ao, Kana-loa, and others introduced the Catholic religion which corrupted the Polynesian religion. The 'aumakua, therefore, became corrupted to a guardian angel that was the deified soul of one departed, and was like a canonized saint called upon for assistance. Of course, this theory would be hard to prove or disprove."

The term *'aumakua* is derived from the word *akua*. Hawaiians believed in many *akua*, who were gods and goddesses such as Kane, Ku and Lono. There was also a belief in the concept that mortal men and women, once deceased, could become gods and goddesses. These types of gods and goddesses were of a lesser degree of power than that of the *akua*, nevertheless, they were worshipped just the same.

The *'aumakua* were very important to a family, who would pray to them to ask for help and guidance. The *'aumakua* manifested themselves throughout the natural world. They could be found in plants, animals or in geological form.

Young boys and girls were required to learn all about the names and forms taken by their family *'aumakua* by the time they were seven years old so that they may be careful not to offend or harm any of them.

Two of the most common outer manifestations, or *kinolau*, the *'aumakua* took were as sharks or as giant gecko-type lizards, or *mo'o*. If a family had a shark *'aumakua*, for example, then the shark would be sacred to that particular family so they would be treated with the utmost respect and would not be eaten. There are several legendary accounts of sharks saving Hawaiians with shark *'aumakua* from peril in the sea.

Another way to look at this concept is that these creatures were sacred to the people because they were literally seen as "*'ohana*" (family).

Offerings were made to them and they were called in during times of need to assist struggling family members.

Supposedly the *'aumakua* would often hover in spirit around the heads of the family members, which could be where Long got the idea of locating the *'aumakua* at the head, or spiritual center of the person.

Pele is perhaps the most famous example of an *'aumakua*, or ancestor god. At one time, Pele was a real person who was said to have come to Hawaii from the island of Bora Bora in the 13th century, although opinions differ as to her exact homeland. People still worship her today. One Hawaiian group, mentioned earlier, called The Edith Kanakaole Foundation admits to having several members who continue to worship Pele today. They have an interesting site on the web with stories of hula, chanting, and the legend of Pele.

Uhane

In Hawaiian, *uhane* is defined as "a ghost or appari-
tion." According to Pali Lee, this word is seldom used
in the Hawaiian language. *Uhane* were spirits or souls
of the deceased, or ghosts. In Long's interpretation,
uhane was man's conscious mind, which resided in his
solar plexus region.

Uhane could refer to the soul that leaves the body
at death, or it may refer to an actual ghost or earthbound soul who is trapped here and separated from the
eternal bliss of heaven.

At death, Hawaiians believed people would be met
by their *'aumakua* who would escort them into the
afterlife. If a mortal man offended his *'aumakua*
during his lifetime, he would become *uhane*. As such,
his *'aumakua* would abandon him by not meeting him
at death to accompany him in to heaven. He or she
would be doomed to roam the earth forever as a lost
soul of sorts.

Many of these earthbound souls were said to have
marched together during certain times of the year and
the Hawaiians have a legend of these lost souls, calling
them the "night marchers."

Apparently large processions of *uhane* march
through the streets at night and will kill any mortal man
who happens to walk in their path. Today, there is still talk
of this phenomenon on the islands.

Long mentions the definition of *uhane* as ghosts,
but simply took the concept a few steps beyond the
actual definition by naming it the conscious mind.

Unihipili

In Huna, the *unihipili* is the term for man's unconscious mind; according to Long, it is through the *unihipili* that one learns to communicate to the high self to manifest desires and prayers.

Long said he developed this concept based on his interpretation of the definitions of various root words he found in the *Hawaiian Dictionary*. The problem with this is that *"unihipili"* is not a common word, and Long said he constructed it by piecing together several root words to arrive at his conclusion for what this means. How he could have constructed his definition of the *unihipili* as subconscious mind is beyond my scope of reasoning.

Long used the following roots to construct the meaning of *unihipili*: The first, *"u"* which means "to grieve," according to Long and the *Hawaiian Dictionary*. However, it has many other meanings as well.

The next part is *"nihi"* which Long said means "gods." When I looked it up in the dictionary however, it said the meaning is "creeping silently and softly." And the third aspect of the word is *"pilli"* which Long said means "to cling or stick."

The *unihipili*—also called an *uhinipili*,—is a "dreadful spirit summoned by a *kahuna*." It was apparently a dead child or fetus used in ceremonial practices. Both *unihipili* and *uhinipili* are very uncommon words, and neither is found in the dictionary.

According to Kelsey's letter to Long:

> *"An* unihipili *is a deified fetus of a once-human soul. A piece of bone, or some relic of*

*the deceased was called upon in spirit, thus
creating a living entity in spirit form, which was
sent on missions of evil, generally revenge or
death, by its keeper ('U =sad, nihi=to sneak by,
pili=to attach to a person)."*

In Huna, Long defines the word *unihipili* as man's
unconscious mind, claiming it is only through building
rapport with our *unihipili* that we may send thoughts to
the high self for actualization.

Of all the words Long used to create the Huna
system, this one is probably most off the mark as far as
the actual definition of the word is concerned.

Unihipili is a rather complex topic and little
information is written on it. Apparently, if a young
baby dies, or a woman miscarries, the remains were
sometimes put to ritualistic use and deified. A ritualistic ceremony involving a very specific process was
performed to accomplish this.

First, the skin was removed from the body and the
hair and bones were kept. The remains were wrapped
in *kapa*, a Hawaiian handmade bark cloth used in
ritual, and kept inside the person's house.

If the person wanted to please the particular family
'aumakua, they may take part of the remains to some
significant place relating to that *'aumakua*. For example, for the shark *'aumakua*, they may take part of
the remains to the ocean. For *mo'o* (the lizard) they
may take it to the top of a mountain.

Similar to Dr. Frankenstein creating his monster in the
lab, the power (*mana*) of the *unihipili* could then be called
on by its maker, usually for less-than-virtuous purposes.

Another explanation for this obscure concept is that
the *unihipili* are spirits who are persuaded to stay around

to provide service to the "master" who created them. This explanation implies the *unihipili* may be created from a deceased adult as opposed to simply being a child, infant, or fetus.

By gathering the parts as before mentioned, and bundling them in *kapa* (bark cloth), these spirits will take on the qualities and characteristics of whoever made them, whether good or evil.

The *unihipili* requires continual care and maintenance. Without proper treatment, it may turn on its creator. The creator, or master, is responsible for "feeding" the spirit whatever it desires and providing it with *awa* (kava-kava drink). Again, if the new creation is denied in any way, it could potentially destroy the master.

There is nothing positive about this concept and I find it amazing that Long was able to construct his definition of an unconscious mind from that particular word.

In *The Secret Science Behind Miracles*, Long explains that the grasshopper is a symbol for the unconscious mind. He may have concluded this based on the *Hawaiian Dictionary* definition of the word *'uhini*, which means "grasshopper" in Hawaiian.

The poor interpretation of this concept leads me to believe that Long must have seen this word in some ancient Hawaiian chants and decided to adopt it to his system. It makes one wonder exactly what type of chants he was reading, though, because of the dark nature of the subject matter.

Mana

Long went into great depth to describe the differing levels of *mana*, or spiritual power of a person. He defined them as *mana*, *mana-loa* and *mana-mana*. *Mana* was used by the unconscious mind, *mana-mana* by the conscious mind, and *mana-loa* by the higher self. How he constructed the three level system is beyond me.

To the Hawaiians, *mana* is personal power, like charisma, that you are born with or you acquire through schooling and apprenticeship.

It is the same concept as universal life force described by Baron Eugene Ferson.

In this interpretation, Long was most correct. Even the Hawaiian people in their writings speak of the fact that there are some people who are simply born with greater amounts or levels of *mana*. In ancient Hawaiian culture, these people were usually of the *ali'i*, or priestly class. All rulers – kings, queens, princes and princesses – were born of the *ali'i*. In fact, most *kahuna* were also of the *ali'i*.

In ancient times, families were very concerned with keeping the *mana* strong; to this end, many marriages were arranged so that people would marry within the family to keep the *mana* as pure as possible.

Everything has *mana*, according to Hawaiian culture – not only people, but everything in nature as well. The life-giving ocean, fish, birds, plants and all animals carried their own unique *mana*. Everything in nature was sacred to some extent and was seen as a blessing to be thankful for.

In the *Hawaiian Dictionary*, *loa* means "very much," so Long's definition of *mana-loa* appears to be somewhat accurate.

Ha

In Huna the "*ha*" was a type of breathing used to raise the *mana* in the body. This is a very powerful technique, primarily because many people in society today do not breathe properly. Any conscious effort to maximize and slow the breath is bound to have health benefits.

In Hawaiian culture, the *ha* was actually a rite performed by a *kahuna* on his or her deathbed.

The *kahuna* would take on students to learn his craft. One comparable example could be that of a canoe builder. One person in the group would excel at this craft and they would become the *kahuna* of canoe building. During his life while training students, there may be one or two who would excel in the craft and from those the *kahuna* would choose who would receive the final secret.

The concept was that the *kahuna* would share much of his knowledge with the students, but would not share everything. That is why he or she could remain in power and have a place of prestige in society.

When the *kahuna* felt his death was imminent, he would call the student whom he had chosen to be his successor to the deathbed, speak the final secret into his ear, and breathe his *mana* into the students' mouth with a "*ha*" sound.

If the chosen one did not want to accept the gift of *mana*, as would occasionally happen, the *kahuna* may have a second choice of a student to whom he would pass on the knowledge. This was a rare occurrence, however, since receiving *mana* was a high honor according to Hawaiian culture.

In Long's work, he felt the *ha* breath must be passed in sets of four. This may have been due to the fact that the word "*ha*" means "four" according to the *Hawaiian Dictionary*. The number four was a very symbolic and sacred number to the Hawaiian people—and to many other native cultures—as it is the number of the seasons and the directions.

Aka

In Huna, *aka* is the shadowy body, or etheric double, of a person. It could also refer to the concept of an *aka* cord, the energetic cord that connects people to everything they touch or own. In the *Hawaiian Dictionary*, *aka*, as Long states, means "shadow or reflection."

The notion of an *aka* cord could have come from the term *kala*, which means "to cut loose, or free." This term implies a cord, which may be where the modern-day Huna practitioners came up with the next concept.

Ho'oponopono

Ho'oponopono literally means "to correct." From information found in Long's original work, modern day Huna practitioners created their version to this process (the Hawaiian code of forgiveness) which was mentioned earlier. The concept was based on Long's description of *aka* cords that are connected to all living and inanimate objects.

In order to be free and to allow life force to become

maximized, it is necessary to cut cords with everything and everyone one encounters.

This theory is strikingly similar to a technique used in modern-day psychotherapy of cord cutting, where the client is asked to cut cords with people who need to be forgiven. This exercise can be very empowering and healing.

This philosophy was created out of two concepts which will be discussed here in detail: true *ho'oponopono* and the process of *kala*, which means "to loosen or untie."

In ancient Hawaii as well as in modern times, *ho'oponopono* was a process engaged in by the entire *'ohana* (family).

If someone in the family was ill or upset, the entire family would gather for several hours, aided by a facilitator, to discuss the problem, possible causes, and arrive at a solution.

The counselor would work with everyone to help family members air feelings and arrive at a conclusion as to why the illness or problem was present.

For example, if someone was sick, the family would begin by first discussing the patient's feelings, uncovering any hidden anger or hostility he or she may be feeling due to a misunderstanding.

Then each family member would be allowed to speak. In between each person's talk there would be a period of silent reflection where everyone could internalize and ponder what was being said.

Often, it was discovered that one of the family members was harboring resentment toward the sick person, often outside of their conscious awareness, as this was a process of the unconscious mind.

Eventually, an explanation could be determined.

Perhaps there were hurt feelings after another member of the family may have said something that was misunderstood.

Then the process of *kala* would take place in which family members would release the person by forgiving their unintentional transgressions.

By forgiving each other, Hawaiians believed they were able to use more of their *mana* toward productive purposes so peace and harmony could be quickly restored to the family unit.

Kahuna

According to Long, *kahuna* means "carpenter" in Hawaiian. In actuality, his definition was in error. The *Hawaiian Dictionary* lists the word carpenter as "*kamana.*"

In the Hawaiian culture, there are many, many types of *kahuna*. Three of the most common are:

'ana-'ana – Most people who study Hawaiian spirituality find themselves most preoccupied with this class of *kahuna*. They were known as the sorcerers, the "death dealing" *kahuna* who were trained in the art of praying others to death. Contrary to popular belief, this was actually seen as a very noble profession. The *kahuna 'ana-'ana* usually used their abilities to wage war against enemies to defend and honor their own kingdoms. Rather than creating bloody battlefields, kings would simply have their enemies destroyed in this less violent manner. The *kahuna* were bound under strict ethical and moral guidelines concerning the use of discretion in their practices. They were often involved in healing the ill as well, and could counteract attacks made on their people using healing prayers. Should the *kahuna* stray from his ethics and use the gift for evil purposes, it was considered black magic and he would be deemed among the lowest level of all *kahuna*.

The training for such men was bleak and involved total isolation from society for long periods of time. The training involved the *kahuna* subjecting himself to many hardships, including ingestion of many poisonous plants that would kill the common man. The *kahuna 'ana-'ana* had to become immune to that which would easily kill others. A fascinating account of how this training may have been and what the life of such a man could be like is found in the classic book *The People of Old* by Komakau.

la'au lapa'au – One of the highest orders of *kahuna* who used herbs, plants and prayers for healing. Herbs, flowers and plants were nearly always used in most forms of healing in ancient Hawaii. The *kahuna la'au lapa'au* would arrive at the home of a sick person and begin gathering the necessary items to be used in healing, each having a specific spiritual significance. An entire book could be written on this subject alone, and in fact several have. From what I could gather, this *kahuna* was one of the most important members of the culture and played a key role in society due to the incredible knowledge they possessed of the medicinal uses of the indigenous species of the area.

pule – prayer priest. This *kahuna* was responsible for the prayers and chants used in healing, and in some ways may be compared to our modern pastor or priest in a church, due to the fact that they worked in a house of worship, or *heiau.*

Obviously, this brief section barely scratches the surface of the subject of the *kahuna.* In ancient Hawaii, there were hundreds of experts in myriad professions. This list is included merely as an explanation of some of the most common and to discuss those *kahuna* most relevant to this study.

Thirteen
Origin of the African Theory

One of the main components of Long's teachings involved the parallels he interpreted between the Bible and ancient Hawaiian culture. It was Long's opinion that the Hawaiians were direct descendants of the twelve tribes of Israel, who originated in the area of the Sahara desert before migrating to Egypt and later to other places around the globe.

Long bases this assumption of the testimony of a man he calls Reginald Stewart, who may or may not be a real person. Certainly I have found no documentation or proof such a man actually existed, which is one of rhe major criticisms of Long's work.

Long's hypothesis may have been derived from theories proposed by a man named Abraham Fornander.

Fornander

Fornander was born in 1812 in Oland, Sweden, received his education in Stockholm, and may have been working as a whaler when he traveled the seas and eventually found himself in Hawaii. For a *ha'ole*, Fornander was able to gain incredible political clout and power after marrying Hawaiian Princess Pinao Alanakapu of Molokai. He entered into politics, and served as a judge in Maui for quite some time, donating to charities and serving as a pillar of the community.

Fornander fell out of grace with the Hawaiian people when he wrote a book which continues to be a thorn in the side of many cultural Hawaiians: *An Account of the Polynesian Race: Its Origins and Migrations*, published in 1877. In this legendary three-volume work, Fornander proposes that the Polynesian people are descendants of Israel and Egypt, specifically the twelve tribes of Israel. From the time of its initial publication, it was of great offense to the local people.

Fornander was able to redeem himself somewhat when he wrote *Collection of Hawaiian Antiquities and Folklore* in 1916, which established him as a scholar and interpreter for many of the old Hawaiian myths and legends.

Fornander biographer, Elenor Harmon Davis, wrote about Fornander's Polynesian origins theories in a sort of public relations effort to redeem his tarnished name, claiming that the book was misunderstood by the public, and that Fornander was simply noting similarities between Biblical and Polynesian legends.

My theory is that Long may have read Fornander and developed the idea that the Hawaiians were indeed direct descendants of the twelve tribes of Israel. It is peculiar that in *The Secret Science Behind Miracles*, Long does not even mention Fornander in his book; however, I find it hard to believe he never encountered the work. The proposal Long makes regarding the Hawaiian origins are strikingly similar to those suggested by Fornander some 70 years prior.

Heyerdahl

Theories about the origins of the Polynesian people have been continually debated over the years. For some time, great consideration was given to hypotheses of Thor Heyerdahl. The famed explorer from Norway expostulated that the Polynesian people migrated from Peru and British Columbia based on his study of the tradewinds off the Pacific Ocean and the similarities he noticed between many of the Peruvian and Polynesian carvings. Heyerdahl suggested the first wave of immigrants came from Peru and the second from British Columbia centuries later, and set out to prove his theory by building a raft made of balsa and successfully sailing from Peru to Archipelago. The completion of the trip of over 4,000 miles suggested that the ancient vessels thought to have transported people to Polynesia, while rudimentary, were nevertheless extremely seaworthy.

Since his hypothesis was first introduced to the world in 1941 through papers, and later in Heyerdahl's book *American Indians in the Pacific*, published in 1952, other explanations about Polynesian origin have taken its place as most accepted among genealogists and scholars.

Abraham Fornander: A Biography, written by Davis in 1979, defends Fornander by acknowledging what Davis said was his true opinion of the Polynesian origin-they first migrated to that region from the Malay Archipelago.

Based on extensive studies of genealogical evidence, the generally accepted theory today is that an Indo-Malay people migrated to Polynesia via the Marquessas and Tahiti.

Fourteen
Berbers and the Story of Reginald Stewart

So what about the Berbers in Africa and does this theory hold any validity? As mentioned earlier, one of the major criticisms of Long's work was the story he told about the British man named Reginald Stewart, who supposedly wrote to him about meeting a tribe of Berbers in North Africa who spoke a language similar to that of the Hawaiians. This letter and the relationship Long said he developed with Stewart is what started Long's whole theory about Jesus being a *kahuna*, and is why some Huna followers believe Huna is the teaching of the twelve tribes of Israel.

Reviewers of Long's books, including Albert Palmer, criticized this part of *The Secret Science Behind Miracles* because there is no documentation whatsoever to support whether or not Stewart was a real person.

Later in the book I will reveal a verbatim conversation I had with the spirit of Max, who said yes, Stewart was a real person, yet the question of the validity of the story Long told about him remains. I have no way to adequately research this point since the name "Stewart" in England is as common as "Smith" or "Jones" in the United States.

Who are the Berbers, and how could they possibly

connected to the Polynesian culture?

The term "Berber" refers to a tribe of Africans located in the Atlas Mountains in the northern part of the continent. Early in their history, the Berbers lived in an area expanding from the Atlantic into Egypt until the 7th century when they were pushed by Arab invaders into the Atlas Mountains. Today, they continue to live in the Atlas Mountains and Sahara desert.

Berber also refers to the Afro-Asiatic language the people speak in the areas of Morocco and Tunesia; it can be broken down into several hundred different dialects, most of which are of oral tradition and are not written down.

Due to the Arab influence in this ethnically diverse area of the world, the population is primarily Muslim, so today, the term "Berber" is usually used to describe the language as opposed to the race of people. In their native tongue, the Berber people refer to themselves and their language as *Amazigh*.

There is a theory that the Berber people may have originated from the Libyan Amazon region of the world, hence the similarity between the words "Amazigh" and "Amazon."
Interestingly, it was the Berber women who were literate and knew how to write. They were gifted with the knowledge of their alphabet, called *Tinfinagh*. This would somewhat support the Reginald Stewart story since he claimed the "*kahuna*" of the tribe was a woman, and it is apparent women were keepers

After making a comparison between the Amazigh and Hawaiian languages, however, I feel there is little evidence to suggest the two are at all related.

The following is a poem written in Amazigh:

The Berbers and the Story of Reginald Stewart

A' Vava,

t'wucemd'iyi d'ggudif
teridd tamziw d'eg'qurdac
mi kestaqs'agh a'felhif
tenigh de'zzahr i'wulac

tekradded t'ttaafaradd
avridd nejjran wiyadd
kra ig'dizin teritt d'accpadd
ul nagh yebbu yerna i'ccadd

aghdifk rebi ayen nuklal
ama d'averkan nagh d'amelal
'zzay am'uzal nagh d'aggurcal
ma'tsasa tamcumt yeffghazd wuqlal

MCrif

Now we will look at an ancient Hawaiian chant:

E Lea,
E ku'u akua,
'Eia wau ke 'oki nei i ku'u la'au koa.
Nana pono mai 'oe i ku'u ko'i

Malaila 'oe 'e ho 'opili mau ai.
'A 'ole 'oe 'e ho 'opa kua.
'A 'ole 'oe 'e ho 'ohina i ku'u la'au
Iluna o ka pu 'ulu koa 'e ulu nei.
Ho 'ohina a 'e 'oe ma kahi mala 'ela 'e.
'A 'ole no ho 'i 'oe 'e hou 'ia i kuu la'au.

Na Pule Kahiko – Ancient Hawaiian Prayers, p. 76.

Based on this comparison of the language structure of the two poems, which have no similarities, it is my opinion that, although Stewart may have been a real person, the letter to Long and/or the contents of such a letter may indeed be fictitious.

Fifteen
Healing Symbols

One of the first things Max told me when he came to visit was that I must stop using the Huna healing symbols I had learned in my class. I did so, reluctantly at first, but soon realized the value of the advice.

I was extremely puzzled as to why Max would make such a request, so I decided to do some research into the meaning behind them. I discovered the symbols evoke Uli, sorcery goddess, which was not a completely new discovery because I read that in a book written by the man who "discovered" them. What I did not understand about Uli prior to my research, was that she was the goddess evoked and used by the *kahuna 'ana-'ana* during the death prayers.

It seemed clear to me that it was wise to discontinue using these symbols, not that they are actually tied to death wishes, but because they are named for Uli; the intent behind them could not be in my best interest, as far as I was concerned.

I decided to investigate the symbols Max showed me to see if they were actually Hawaiian. When I first saw them they had a glowing light around them. Max asked me to look at the old ones and compare them. There was a huge difference! The others seemed dark to me, and this was prior to my full knowledge about what they were.

Still, as I looked into this project, I wanted to find some confirmation from cultural Hawaiians about the use of healing symbols.

The Hawaiian people have confirmed they have never used healing symbols. In all of the books I read, I found healing to be done primarily through the *'aumakua*, and through the use of chanting, prayer, and medicinal herbs.

Many people have attempted to relate the petroglyphs found on the islands to healing symbols. Although Hawaiian people told me there is no such connection, it is my opinion that there are healing energies associated with Hawaiian petroglyphs. It will take further research into this area before making any definitive arguements for or against this theory.

The symbols Max showed me seem similar to images found on petroglyphs, and I have witnessed the healing power of the intent behind them; therefore, I am inclined to believe it is something worth looking into in the future.

Sixteen
What About Wicca?

Now we come to the question I asked myself at the beginning of the project. Is Huna indeed a form of Wicca?

One thing is clear to me: Max Freedom Long was a master at taking the best and leaving the rest when it comes to all things metaphysical. He was clearly an avid student of paranormal and psychical sciences and seems to have taken bits and pieces out of many teachings in order to create Huna.

This is evident in his many books where he introduces a subject, and then ties in the *kahuna* to any psychical science topic he is discussing. One example is "The Significance of Seeing into the Future in the Psychometric Phenomenon and in Dreams," Chapter IX in *The Secret Science Behind Miracles*. In this chapter, Long discusses the *kahuna* and then mentions his trip to a séance, which he somehow ties in to the original discussion. In the next chapter, he goes into a dialogue about crystal gazing and precognitive dreams of his parents, then cleverly ties it all in so it somehow relates back to the mysteries of the *kahuna*.

Everything from Dr. Brunler's biometer used in the psychometry studies to the Cameron Aurameter are explored both directly and indirectly under the auspices of Huna.

As I said before, I believe Max was an incredibly creative writer, and was obviously brilliant when it comes to practical use of knowledge he gathered from many sources.

In order to adequately answer the question of how Huna may or may not relate to Wicca, we must first take a brief look at some of the fundamental beliefs of paganism and the Wiccan religion. Paganism refers to the oldest group of earth religions and cultures that are polytheistic in nature, meaning they worship more than one god or deity. This could refer to the Native American cultures, ancient Egypt, Greece, and even the ancient Hawaiian culture, to name a few.

Within the realm of paganism, there are several different sects, Wicca being one.

The Wiccans believe in the respect and worship of nature and the seasons, and in astrology. They consider the goddess (feminine) to be equal to or greater in importance than the god (masculine) part of humanity.

The principle fundamentals of Wiccan faith are the concepts of "three by three," meaning what you send out will come back to you three times, and the phrase "An' it harm none, do what thou wilt."—in other words, do unto to others as you would have them do unto you. The spells in Wiccan faith are merely prayers tied in with much ritual and are not done with evil intent, as some critics say, but are done with the highest good of all concerned.

This is by no means meant to clearly define a complicated belief system in a short space; my intent here is to briefly explain the general beliefs of the religion.

On the other hand, Huna, as it was created by Max

Freedom Long, was never originally intended to be a religion. Long himself was a devout Christian. The painstaking efforts he took to compare Jesus to the *kahuna* suggest, if anything, that Long intended this system to follow more closely with the Christian religion, and to complement it, rather than to be associated with any pagan belief system. The breathing exercises were just that—exercises—and were not seen as spells or charms.

Since Wiccans proclaim to work magic through ritualistic candle-burning and the preparation of herbal remedies, perhaps Long's use of the term "magic" led people to believe Huna is a form of Wicca. In my personal experience with Huna classes, our instructor combined the science of Neuro-Linguistic Programming (created by Richard Bandler) with some pagan practices such as ritualistic burning of prayers, similar to those found in Wiccan candle magic ceremonies.

In addition, we meditated with stones and were asked to concentrate on them, to "become one" with them. This teaching seemed more along the lines of Shamanism to me, and had Native American undertones. I did not, however, see what it had to do with Huna per se, because the stones we used were not even indigenous to Hawaii.

I must also add here that after reading all of Long's books, listening to his tapes and perusing many of his letters to the HRA that in no place did Long discuss activities such as the ones previously described here, at least not that I have seen.

As humans, we enjoy categorizing and labeling things because it seems the only way we can make sense of them is through the comparison of concepts and ideas we already know. It is not always the best thing to do, but it is how we cope with the world around us.

If we must assign a label to various teachings, it would be safer to conclude that the ancient Hawaiian culture could be seen as a form of paganism due to the polytheistic beliefs and the unwavering respect and honoring of nature through the various *'aumakua*.

Based on this information and my own opinions, I feel it is safe to say that *some* modern Huna practitioners have changed the original teachings of Long, and have added Wiccan beliefs into their practices. I do not believe Huna was originally meant to be Wiccan; however, based on new interpretations of Long's work, that perception is certainly valid. Therefore, the answer to the original question is yes, Huna could be described as a far-removed form of Wicca.

Seventeen
Huna in the Spiritual Healing Practice

Like many modern Huna practitioners, I have taken what I have learned in classes and books and combined the various techniques to create my own unique type of therapeutic intervention to use with clients.

The Huna techniques I implement in my work have been extremely helpful to my clients, according to their feedback.

The Huna-based philosophy I implement most often in my work is the modern-day version of *ho'oponopono*, or cord cutting. I have taken Long's teachings and developed my own version of this process.

Through guided imagery, I have people create a stage in their minds. Every person they have ever known is invited to come out on the stage. To jog their memories, I verbally take them through their lives and then at the end, have their unconscious mind,(or *unihipili*, according to Long) go ahead and put anyone on stage they may have consciously forgotten.

If there is anyone there who needs to be forgiven, I ask the person to invite him or her to step to the front of the stage. I have them imagine the one who angered them giving them a sincere, heart-felt apology and telling them that they did not mean to be hurtful, but were only doing the best they could at the time.

If necessary, I have the client apologize to that person as well for any wrong doings, and if necessary, embrace the person.

Then I have them visualize, or "notice," the shadowy (*aka*) cord that extends from their solar plexus and fans out to each person on the stage. Next, using a "giant pair of scissors," they are asked to cut the cords with everyone there, and notice how much more energy (*mana*) they have than they did before.

(Note: I do not actually use Hawaiian terms with clients because I feel it would cause unnecessary confusion. I am using them here since we are discussing Huna fundamentals and I am attempting to demonstrate how these may be applied.)

One woman described the process this way: "When I cut the cord, I felt really dizzy. It took a few minutes, but then I started to feel like I had more energy. It was amazing. I had no idea that I was giving all of my energy away to other people."

I created my own version of *ho'oponopono*. It seems to be very effective for most people, and is the one I use in my practice.

This exercise is easy to do on your own. To do it, you may either have a friend read the following steps to you, or you may take this and record it on a tape and play it for yourself. Your unconscious mind loves to hear the sound of your voice.

Cord Cutting Exercise

First, imagine yourself in a beautiful room. Look around and see what is there. Are there light fixtures? Stairs? Carpet, tile or wood floors? Notice everything about this room.

Next, imagine a doorway in front of you. When you are ready, open the door and step inside.

You will notice a stage in front of you. Go ahead and sit in the seats, if there are any, and begin to focus your attention on this stage.

Imagine the curtain coming back, or a doorway opening up on the stage. Ask your unconscious mind, (*unihipili*) to begin inviting everyone you have ever known to the stage.

Begin with your family. Your parents, regardless of whether they are alive or deceased; brothers, sisters, have them all come out.

Next invite any relatives: aunts, uncles, cousins, step brothers and sisters. Then close family friends or neighbors you had growing up. (Remember: the size of the stage is unlimited so imagine it is big enough to hold *everyone* you know.)

Now begin with kindergarten. See, feel or imagine your friends and teachers coming out to the stage. Then the first grade. See your classmates, teachers, and other people who may have worked in the school. Next the second grade, third, fourth. (Pause in between each grade so you give adequate time to invite everyone out.) Now the fifth, sixth, seventh, eighth, ninth, tenth, eleventh and twelfth. If it applies, place people at your college or university on the stage. Take as long as you need to continue inviting everyone out to the stage.

Now think of people at church, or any neighbors or family friends you may also need to invite. Again, take your time.

As a young adult, think of friends, teachers, employers, co-workers and everyone you have ever known as an adult.

You may even want to include family pets and significant belongings, as they can also be a drain of your life force (*mana*).

Continue this process until everyone is there. When you have finished recalling people, ask your unconscious mind to allow anyone else you may have consciously forgotten to go ahead and step out to the stage.

When everyone is in place, invite those you need to forgive, or who need to forgive you, to step out in front of the crowd.

One by one, imagine talking to these people. Imagine your higher self speaking to their higher selves. Imagine you could thank them for helping you to learn your lessons here on the physical plane. Imagine they could apologize to you for any wrongdoing and explain to you that they did not mean to cause you harm or hurt. In their own way, they were only doing the best they knew how based on their current circumstances.

Imagine you could forgive them and imagine them from a higher perspective as the infinite being of love and light that they are.

Now you may want to apologize to them for any wrongdoing you may have done and explain that you were only doing your best at the time.

Now if you feel it appropriate, you may wish to embrace the person as a gesture of pure forgiveness.

Now imagine you can notice that there is a cord of light that extends from your solar plexus and attaches to the other person at their solar plexus.

Go ahead and notice that, and realize that you are both giving up much of your own vital force *(mana)* by allowing this cord to remain attached. In a moment, we are going to cut this cord.

(Many people have a hard time with this concept. They feel that they could not possibly cut a cord of connection to a loved one. They think it will create a feeling of separation that they could not possibly endure. Let me say to you that this is not the case!

Just as magnetic force attracts, the cutting of the cord creates a kind of magnetism that allows the person to want to reconnect with you and will ultimately create a stronger bond than before! It creates a feeling of wanting to be close and connected.

Think of it as a benevolent act you can do for another. It truly is a gift you can give in the spirit of unselfishness and in the spirit of having a healthy, loving relationship.

The need to feel connected and the fear that may come from the separation is an illusion partly brought on by the way many of us have grown up in codependent, unhealthy relationships. Just try this and see how healing it can be! Take my word for it; this technique can really aid in your relationships!

This concept is called "healing the part of YOU that is another person." The only person in this world who you have any control over whatsoever is YOU. When you heal YOU, then you will change the unconscious projections you put on others, thus changing their behavior toward you. It is really amazing stuff!)

So now that you have noticed this cord between the

two of you, continue to notice it for just a minute longer. I want you now to ask the person if they have anything that belongs to you and to give it back now. (Many times you may find they have a piece of your heart, your whole heart, or maybe a "virtue" of yours such as your dignity, respect, etc.) Imagine that you ask them to give back what belongs to you and see them holding it out in front of you, or if you cannot visualize, just feel it, or hear them tell you what it is, or just have an inner knowing of what they are returning.

Take it by extending your hands; now, imagine yourself putting it back inside. You may even want to physically put your hands out and draw them into your heart area as you bring that missing piece of yourself back inside.

Imagine that you can feel an energetic shift as you integrate this part of yourself back into the whole. You may feel a wave of energy, or a rush of some kind. You may hear a sound or see a mental picture as you reconnect with a part of yourself that may have been missing.

Now see if you have anything that belongs to them. If so, imagine yourself holding it out for them to take back. See, feel or imagine them taking it from you and putting it inside.

Imagine you can notice the relief you now feel and the weight that has been lifted as you let go of this burden and give back what you have been carrying around with you. Imagine it as if the weight of the world has suddenly been lifted from your shoulders. Feel the relief!

When the exchange is finished, I want you to imagine a giant pair of scissors coming out and cutting the cord. Go ahead now and cut the cord between you.

As you do, imagine seeing, feeling or imagining a beam of pure white light coming from above and pouring in the ends of these cut cords on both you and the other person.

Imagine the white light can go into your body through your solar plexus and heal you. Feel the light as it travels down your stomach into your intestines, into your legs – your thighs, knees, ankles, feet, toes. Imagine it traveling up into your heart and healing any cracks. If your heart was missing or broken in any way, imagine the white light healing your heart until it is perfectly healed and whole. Imagine the white light as a laser beam that can run over the heart and heal it so that it is as good as new. Feel the difference as you heal your heart.

Allow the healing light to travel into your arms, neck and head and feel it, almost like a tingling sensation as it travels up your body.

See the other person receiving this same kind of healing. Then imagine the white light becoming so strong that it just lifts the other person and carries them to God or spirit. Wish them well and send them Godspeed as they go into the light and love.

Now repeat this process on any other people who you invited to come to the front of the stage. This may take awhile, but it is very powerful and energizing. It will add years to your life!

When you are finished with these special people, imagine you can once again stand back and look at all of the people on that stage.

Now I want you to imagine that you could notice looking down or feeling that there is a big cable of light coming from your solar plexus region. Notice how it fans out in so many directions into little thread-like cords that are attached to everyone on that stage. Can you see it? Great!

Now in a moment, we are going to cut all of these cords. So go ahead and imagine seeing the big pair of scissors and see it coming near you and cutting that cable in your solar plexus.

As you do this, I hope you are sitting down because you will probably feel a rush of energy! It may make you dizzy!

(The first time I did this I literally fell out of my chair! I could not believe how much lighter I felt instantly, and it caused me to lose touch with gravity for a moment! You cannot imagine how much energy you are giving away until you try this process!)

See the huge beam of white light and allow it to heal you and all others on the stage. Allow the white light to move through you as it did before. Take your time and allow any healing to take place that needs to.

Now see those souls being carried up, up and away to spirit as you wish them all well and thank them for being a part of your evolutionary experience.

****

What is amazing about doing this is that when you are finished you have really healed yourself *and* the other people involved. Although they will not consciously know it, on an unconscious level they will get this and feel it in some way. It may come to them as a feeling that they need to contact you or talk to you.

When I did the process the first time, I really did fall out of my chair, which was amazing. But what was even more uncanny than that was the fact that over the next week I began to hear from people via the phone and Internet who I had literally not talked to in five years or more. Suddenly these people were contacting me trying, like I said before, to reconnect with me. It was a great gift to hear from so many people, which is why I said this process is a blesing because it really does create the need to reconnect which ultimately establishes closeness that would not have been possible otherwise. As I said, some of these people I had not talked to in years and would not have needed to talk to them, nor would they have needed to talk to me unless this had happened! It works!

159

Eighteen
Case Studies

Cord cutting can be an extremely powerful process for grief recovery. Oftentimes, we have a hard time letting go of those who are gone. This can sap the life force from us and distract us from doing what it is we have come to do here. Additionally, it can lead to illness and depression.

I have many clients suffering from grief and I have found a simple way to address the situation and relieve the feeling of loss. I believe some of the pain we feel when we grieve is the panicked desperation we have from being physically separated from our loved ones. The following exercise is an excellent way to relieve that feeling of separation.

I have the person first imagine seeing the lost loved one standing in front of them and have them notice the energetic cord running from their solar plexus to that of the departed loved one. Then I have them imagine they are reaching out to them and holding them and putting them back into their heart. I have them acknowledge the feeling of connection they now feel. Then I explain to them that there is a part of the loved one that will always be with them since the loved one is merely on another plane of existence. We are all a part of this vast universe and we are all connected at all times.

This seems to be very comforting to all of the clients who I have taken through it.

I also explain that at the same time, there is a part of them that needs to let go of the deceased in order to allow both themselves and the loved one to fulfill their soul's purpose and that it will be okay to do so. Then, I have them cut the cord and see the person floating away, sometimes with angels escorting them.

One client came to see me after losing his father. He had been depressed and was suffering from head and backaches. After the reconnecting and cord cutting process, he told me the following: "I felt like I was whole again and everything would be okay. I could see my dad standing there and it was like I could feel him again, as if he was really there. It was a relief. After I cut the cord, I felt like I left my problems behind, which was a real relief. It felt like a weight had been lifted. My back and head did not hurt anymore."

Another woman experienced her deceased parents walking up to her. "When I reached out to them it was so comforting to reconnect with their energy. I felt hot all over. Then when I cut the cords, I felt a rush of energy. Even after the experience, I seem to have more energy now than I did before."

I combine the cord-cutting ideology of Huna with the process called soul retrieval in which you ask people to give back things that belong to you. Particularly in cases of grief, whether it be grief over a death or divorce, this is very empowering.

The same woman who cut cord with her parents described the soul retrieval process. "When I asked them to give back anything they had that belonged to me, both parents gave me my heart. It was interesting that my dad reached out first, although in life it was my mother who seemed more nurturing. After putting my heart back inside, I felt more complete and whole."

Cord cutting can be very powerful in healing relationships of those who are closest to us. One client came to me for a past life regression to find out about her relationship to her mother, who she considered to be needy and who seemed to cling to her in an unhealthy way.

She discovered that in a previous life, her mother was her wife who she abandoned, which could explain her behavior in the current incarnation. After doing a process of soul retrieval in which her mother gave her back her autonomy and she gave her mother freedom, the client found that the relationship on the physical plane had totally changed as a result of this work: "My mother called and began to get going with the same old issues, trying to make me feel guilty about all sorts of things. As soon as she hung up, I told my boyfriend that she had called, and what she said to me. He could not believe how calm I was. I had not even noticed at first, but I *was* calm and I did not react to her in the same way anymore. Now as time goes on and I continue to remain calm, her behavior towards me has completely changed, and our relationship is better than it was before."

Another woman cut cords with her husband and noticed an immediate improvement in the relationship: "A few days after the session, my husband asked me to go to the opera. We had not been out in months!"

As mentioned before, the cord cutting actually creates the magnetism that makes the other person feel they want to reconnect with you. I have seen this over and over again with clients and with myself! This is an extremely powerful technique!

The other part of my practice is energy work using the Huna symbols combined with Reiki and various stones and crystals. I use the energy to balance the chakras and balance the subtle energy system of the client.

Energy work with Huna is not as passive as Reiki. With Reiki, the practitioner asks for energy to begin flowing, and it does. In Huna, one must draw the symbol, and use the breath; then, the energy will flow. Huna feels more powerful to me and seems to create more dramatic shifts in clients in less time than using Reiki alone. Perhaps it is due to the breath.

I started breathing while visualizing the Reiki symbols also, and have found it increases their power as well, although I did not learn it that way in my Reiki classes.

As I mentioned earlier, the discarnate Max told me not to use the original symbols taught to me in my Huna class. Instead, he gave me three, which I now use exclusively.

After discarding the other system, I noticed an immediate shift in the energy, which seemed to become more powerful than before and seemed to yield more amazing results.

I put together a short survey asking clients to describe the sensations they felt during the Huna energy session. For the survey I used only the new Huna energy work in order to be able to objectively evaluate the effects of Huna alone.

One man said the following: "I had a problem with stomach cramps for three days. During my chakra balancing, the pain stopped. My right shoulder has been hurting for almost two years. I could not sleep on that side without pain. Within 48 hours of the session, the pain lessened and I can sleep on that side again."

Because all illness begins in the subtle energy system and eventually reaches the physical body, this client's remarks are not at all surprising. Energy work is used to create change in the energetic part of the person and create perfection there, while removing energetic blockages. After blocks are removed and perfection is established, it can take 24-72 hours for the change to fully manifest in the physical body.

Many clients report drastic improvements within this time frame because it takes that long for the change that has taken place spiritually to reach the physical plane.

Another client reported more positive results: "During the last session, I had a head injury from the night before and my forehead was swollen. After a while, the pain and swelling went away. The headache I had for 16 hours went away also."

And another: "I had been suffering from chronic fatigue, which completely went away. I feel rejuvenated physically, mentally and spiritually."

The same client described the actual sensations during the session: "It was very relaxing and occasionally I felt twitches and tingling sensations. At one point I thought Shelley was gently touching my leg, but when I opened my eyes she was actually standing near my head."

The word "tingling" popped up again and again when people were describing the session. All felt it was a relaxing experience.

Here it is again, step by step, for you to try at home:

Prayer Manifestation Exercise

The other process that several clients have found extremely powerful is the prayer manifestation exercise described in the first part of the book.

Using the breath to assist in focusing intent seems to help actualize goals. Several clients have used this process with positive results.

1. Decide what you would like and write it down in positive language. By positive language, I mean without the use of negatives. Make sure you write it down in a way that asks specifically for what you want instead of what you do not want. For example, you need to say you want a red car instead of saying that you don't want a white car. The unconscious mind has trouble processing negatives and is used to following direct orders. For example, have you ever said to yourself "I hope I don't lock my keys in the car!" or "I hope I don't lose my wallet!" and sure enough, you end up doing just that? I think this has happened to just about everyone and I believe the reason is because your unconscious did not recognize the negative; in essence you just told yourself to lose your wallet and to lock your keys in the car! So beware and take care to write this phrase positively.

2. Phrase it as if you already have it. In Long's work, he suggests that this creates the mental conditioning to allow you to accept the desired outcome as true. In neuro-linguistic program-

ming, this is done in the opposite way: to reach a goal or outcome, you must imagine what you want and see yourself looking out your own eyes at it. Then you must dissociate yourself from the outcome by imagining you are looking at a picture of you getting what you want. This supposedly tells the unconscious mind that it is a desire that is not yet attained so it creates the magnetism that allows you to strive toward that goal.

3. Now, imagine your conscious mind is located in your head. Next, imagine thoughtforms, or mental pictures of what you want, traveling down to your solar plexus, which is the home of your unconscious mind. Then, imagine you can send those same pictures (thoughtforms) up toward the crown of your head, where your higher self (*'aumakua*) resides.

4. You will take ten sets of four breaths each. With each set, imagine the cord going higher toward the crown of the head. By the ninth set of breaths, imagine you have fully connected to the high self and then take the last set of breaths.

5. Now that you are fully connected, pull out the paper where you wrote your desired outcome and read it to yourself or aloud—whichever you prefer—three times. Read it straight off the paper as opposed to trying to memorize it because you want to make sure you plant the seed correctly in proper language.

6. Now reach up to the top of your head in the area of the crown chakra, and imagine pushing the energy of the higher self (which is residing above the head) down inside your body.

7. Say the phrase "My prayer has now taken flight, let the rain of blessings fall." The rain of blessings is a special feeling you have, kind of like the chills that you get when you are really connected to Spirit, or in this case, your higher self. You may know what I mean. It feels like goosebumps all over, as if the wings of angels are brushing you. It is a powerful feeling!

8. Now sit and meditate and allow yourself to imagine that you are now totally connected to your higher self. Allow the high self to present messages to you in the form of symbols and visions for as long as you like.

9. When ready, come back into the room feeling wide awake and refreshed! You may want to jot down any images you received in a journal or notebook so you may use them to help you create your future goal.

10. Repeat this process often, perhaps weekly, depending on the importance of your outcome or goal. By putting your attention on it, the desire will be more likely to become manifest on the physical plane.

Nineteen
The Final Answer

The final answer to my question would arrive with the death certificate of Max Freedom Long from San Diego County, where he lived for several years. I anxiously awaited the arrival of the document to draw my final conclusions to the mystery. Did he indeed kill himself, as was suggested to me earlier?

The certificate proved that he did. On September 23, 1971, Max Freedom Long died at 11:00 p.m. of a self-inflicted gunshot wound to the head. He apparently used a .410 gauge shotgun to commit the act, the only question that still remained was why?

Was Max Freedom Long indeed suffering from a guilty conscience?

That answer would come to me some weeks later after reviewing the autopsy report from the San Diego coroner's office.

The report said Long had been despondent since the death of his wife some four years earlier. At the time of his suicide, Long was also 80 years old and suffering from ill health. The report said a previous suicide attempt had been made on April 14, 1971, when Long unsuccessfully overdosed on barbiturates.

The coroner's report said Long was suffering from terminal osteosarcoma, a form of bone cancer. Appar-

The death certificate of Max Freedom Long.

ently, the cancer was affecting his leg and had become quite crippling and painful.

His recent hopelessness was due to his terminal diagnosis, according to a neighbor who was on the scene after the suicide.

Based on my research and the information Long told me through automatic writing, the suicide was unrelated to past events surrounding Huna.

I had planned to conclude my research at this point, when the discarnate Long urged me to get a copy of the actual suicide note, which I eventually did. After going through some lengths to get it, I can say with certainty that his death was not at all related to Huna.

It was an extremely short, scribbled message on the back of a pharmacy receipt in which Long said he was ready to join his wife in the hereafter. The suicide seems to be known in some Huna circles; however, it is something most practitioners treat as a "dirty little secret," which must be hidden. Therefore, all sorts of misguided theories could be brought forth by people as to why Long would do such a thing.

In our automatic writing sessions, Long told me the reason he has come back is to set the record straight about the origins of Huna and to bring to light the fact that he made the system up using his incredible knowledge of the spiritualist movement and psychical science. It is that, and that alone, that he wished to set straight.

Long's insistence that I obtain the suicide note may have been his way of ending the scandalous rumors surrounding his death, finally after 30 years. Certainly we may be disappointed to learn Long took his own life, but God bless him, we would have to walk a day in his shoes to fully understand his pain.

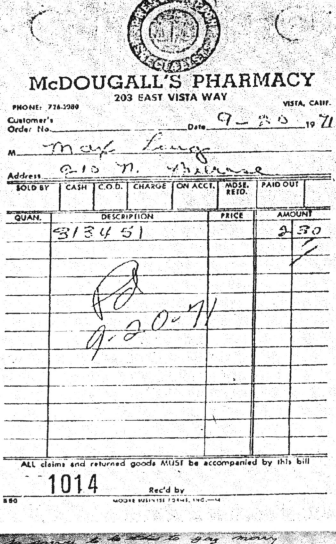

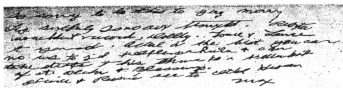

This barely legible suicide note was scribbled on the back of the pharmacy receipt shown above. It does not appear to have anything to do with Huna.

Twenty
What Does Max Have to Say About All This?

I decided after all of this research to call on Max again to answer some direct questions. Following is a transcript of what we discussed.

SK - Did you ever meet Dr. William Tufts Brigham?

MFL - NO

SK - Did you make up Reginald Stewart as well?

MFL - NO

SK - Was he a real person?

MFL - YES, REAL.

SK - Where did you get most of the ideas that you used to create Huna?

MFL - NEW AGE THOUGHT

SK - What specifically?

MFL - SPIRITUALIST MOVEMENT

SK - What do you want to say to the people who have followed you and believed in you?

MFL - SORRY

SK - Sorry for what?

MFL - LYING

SK - Lying about what?

MFL - EVERYTHING

SK - What specifically?

MFL - BRIGHAM, GREED, MAKING UP HUNA

Max Freedom Long at his
home in Vista, California.

SK - Anything else?

MFL - CAN'T CHANGE IT

SK - Change what?

MFL - EVERYTHING

SK - But you do understand that Huna has really helped a lot of people, don't you?

MFL - YES

SK - Are you happy about that?

MFL - YES, (BUT) READY (TO) TELL (THE) TRUTH

Twenty-One
Modern-Day Huna
Conclusion

"Religion is, in reality, the science of the relationship between man and any living beings higher or more evolved than himself who may have an influence on his life either here or hereafter. The science of Huna can and does cover and include all of the items listed above. This would make it so complicated that a mountain of books could not describe it fully."
Max Freedom Long, Self-Suggestion, p. 101.

Huna is an invention of Max Freedom Long, which combines some of the most useful material from many psychical sciences into a unique format that has been helpful to many people.

This research has enabled me to say with certainty that Huna is in no way related to the ancient teachings of the Polynesians.

Today, there are several *"kahuna"* popping up all over the globe, claiming to have the answers to the mysteries of Hawaii.

I find this discouraging, particularly on behalf of the Hawaiian people, who report that many Huna practitioners show up in their homeland professing to know more about their culture than they do.

The answers I have received from my research have led me to conclude that many Huna practitioners in the United States are misinformed about the origins of Huna.

Most courses teach students that Huna is *the* teaching of the ancient Polynesians. This is not the case at all. Huna is one man's interpretation or opinion of what he *believes* was practiced by the ancient *kahuna*. The reality is we simply do not know the truth about what was done because the *kapu* placed on the people after the arrival of the missionaries forced them into silence about their culture and practices. Spirituality was a private matter, a secret, kept amongst family members.

My whole conclusion boils down to one important concept that has shaped much of the world as we know it from the beginnings of time—*faith*.

Any religious, spiritual or metaphysical study works for us because we believe it does. The mind is a powerful thing and the ideas and concepts we have faith and believe in create such a force within us it can move mountains. Huna has a valuable place in the world for those individuals who have found it to work for them.

In the United States, there has long been a tradition of eating black-eyed peas on New Year's Day for good luck. In a recent newspaper article, there was a discussion about a farmer from Athens, Texas, who began growing black-eyed peas in 1947 as a crop because it creates an influx of nitrogen in the soil that aids in crop rotation. The article suggested that the farmer made up the story to sell his peas, which grew in high quantity.

Regardless of the origin of this myth, many U.S. citizens are serving black-eyed peas with the meal on New Year's Day. Why? Because they have become convinced that if they do not consume the dry, speckled, beans their year will not go as well as if they did. *Faith* is what keeps the legend alive. I am inclined to believe they are right. We certainly get what we ask for, and what we expect, so if we think we are having a better year because of a vegetable, then we probably are. That is one perspective. Imagine people having a rather devastating turn of events in a given year and being able to say "Just think how much worse it could've been if we had not had the peas!"

On a similar note, in a recent episode of the CBS television show, *Sunday Morning*, there was a story about "Madame Pele." (Note: the Hawaiians do *not* appreciate having their goddess referred to as "Madame.")

It was an interview with a man from the Parks Department in Kilauea who told about the urban legend of taking lava rocks from Pele's fiery home.

The correspondent interviewed several people who claimed they were cursed with all kinds of bad luck after removing the lava rocks and bringing them back to the mainland. Everything from strange accidents and broken bones to ill health to divorce was being blamed on the "Madame."

Toward the end of the interview, the Kilauea representative admitted the story of Pele's curse was invented by the Parks Department to encourage people to respect the site.

Who knows if there really is a curse or not? I won't be testing the theory myself. I had my black-eyed peas on New Year's Day, and I kept my hands to myself at

Kilauea!

I must admit that on some level the research I have done is personally disappointing, as I expected to find I had truly learned something Polynesian. On the other hand, I am pleased to have discovered an intriguing mystery, the questions about which cannot be definitely answered.

My journey has created a curiosity within me to investigate other indigenous cultures and ancient spiritual practices, which I will report on in the future.

Over the course of this project, I have spent considerable time thinking about the first thing Max ever said to me: God sent him here. I believe that is true. Perhaps Max has been in some form of "spiritual limbo," not because of his suicide (I do not believe suicide is a sin), but because as we say in regression therapy, he may have had some unfinished business to take care of here on the earth-plane. I hope this writing will help him move on in peace.

"Ka hohonu I hiki 'ole ke ana 'ia, aka,
ua 'ike 'ia no kahi mau papa."

The depths have not all been fathomed, but a few reefs have been seen.

Sunset on Waikiki Beach

Hawaiian Glossary

Aka - Literally translates to "shadow." In Huna, this is the etheric double, or shadowy body of a person.

Aka cord - A cord made of etheric substance that emanates from our solar plexus region and attaches to everything and everyone we come in contact with.

Akua - God, goddess, or deity.

Ali'i - The chiefly or ruling class in ancient Hawaii from which all kings, queens and priests come from.

'Aumakua - The deified ancestral spirits of the Hawaiian people. In Huna, it is used to describe the higher self.

Awa - Pure kava-kava root turned into a highly potent, intoxicating drink enjoyed by ancient Hawaiians during rituals and ceremonies as an offering to the gods. The term refers to both the plant root itself, and the drink.

Ha - Literally translates "to breathe, four or fourth." It is a ritual in which a dying kahuna breathes the final secret of his trade to a deserving student who will carry on his teachings after his death. In Huna, it is the term to describe a process of breathing in through the nose and exhaling while simultaneously breathing out of the mouth with a "ha" sound.

Ha'ole - Literally translates to "without breath." The term used to describe the Caucasian settlers to the islands, which is still used today to describe any non-Hawaiian.

Haumea - The mother of all Hawaiians according to Hawaiian mythology.

Heiau - A pre-Christian place of worship, sacred site or temple used in ancient Hawaii to worship the gods.

Hi'aka - Sister to Pele in Hawaiian mythology.

Ho'oponopono - Literally translates "to correct error" this is the Hawaiian process of forgiveness in which a facilitator is called in to a family to discuss any misunderstandings so that peace and harmony can be restored to the family unit. In Huna, it is a process where the client imagines a cord between him/her and other people and imagines forgiving others then cutting the cord between them.

Huna – Literal translation "secret." Process created by Max Freedom Long in the early 1930's used to describe his interpretations of what he supposedly believed the ancient Hawaiian kahuna did in their healing.

Kahuna – (singular and plural) Literally translates to "expert or priest." Term used to describe any highly skilled person in ancient Hawaii who was the expert in his field of study.

> **'ana-'ana** – kahuna skilled in praying others to death. Black magician, sorcerer.

> **la'au lapa'au** – kahuna skilled in administering herbal remedies for various illnesses.

> **pule** – a prayer priest, like a modern pastor.

Kala – Literal translation "to untie, free." This was part of the Ho'o'ponopono process used in ancient Hawaii. After someone is forgiven the process of kala allowed the transgressor to be set free of any guilt.

Kamehamaha The Great – The first and perhaps most famous monarch in Hawaiian history who united the islands under one rule for the first time in 1810.

Kane – One of the four major Hawaiian gods. Kane represented the life force. In Huna, Kane was the representation of the higher self.

Kanaloa - One of the four major gods of Hawaii, he was the companion of Kane and was god of the sea. In Huna, he represented the physical body.

Kapa - Ancient hand-woven Hawaiian bark cloth. Used in ceremonial practices.

Kapu - Taboo, off limits, sacred.

Ki - Plant used in sacred practices and healing. Pronounced *ti*.

Kilauea - Volcano located in the southern part of the island of Hawaii is known as the home of the goddess Pele.

Kinolao - Outer manifestation (usually found in nature) taken by any of the 40,000 gods or goddesses of Hawaii. For example, the god Kane *is* sugar cane. Pele *is* fire.

Ku - One of the four major gods of Hawaii. Ku was god of war to which human sacrifice was occasionally made. In Huna, he represented the unconscious mind.

Laka - Hawaiian goddess of the Hula dance.

Lono - One of the four major Hawaiian gods who provided food to the people. He is a symbol of peace, and was the god that Captain Cook was mistaken for. In Huna, he represents the conscious mind.

Mana - Life force. In Huna, mana is represented by water.

Nui - Great, big, important.

'Ohana - Family.

Pa'ao - Tahitian Priest who arrived in Hawaii between 1100-1250 who became the precursor to all priests in the kahuna nui lineage.

Pele - Goddess of the volcano Kilauea. She was represented as a beautiful young woman or a very old woman. The most famous goddess in Hawaii, she is considered to be an 'aumakua, or deified ancestor to the Hawaiian people.

Pule - A prayer.

Uhane - Hawaiian term for spirit or ghost. In Huna, this was the conscious mind.

Unihipili/uhunipili - A deified soul of someone who was once mortal. In Huna, it is the unconscious mind.

Wai - Water.

Bibliography

Armitage, George. <u>A Brief History of Hawaii.</u>
Waipahu, Hawaii: Hawaiian Service, Inc., 1996.

Beckwith, Martha. <u>Hawaiian Mythology</u>. Honolulu,
HI: University of Hawaii Press, 1970.

Beckwith, Martha Warren. <u>The Kumulipo: A Hawaiian
Creation Chant</u>. Chicago: The University Press, 1951.

Bible, King James Version

"Bishop's Brigham." *The Beacon* v. 4 n. 10, October,
1964.

Brigham, William Tufts. <u>Hawaiian Feather Work</u>.
Honolulu, HI: Bishop Museum Press, 1903.

Brigham, William Tufts. <u>Ms. Sc.Brigham Box 3.27</u>.
Honolulu, HI: Bishop Museum.

Brigham, William Tufts. <u>Ms. Sc.Brigham Box 3.28</u>.
Honolulu, HI: Bishop Museum.

Brigham, William Tufts. Ms. Sc.Brigham Box 4.19.
Honolulu, HI: Bishop Museum.

Brigham, William Tufts. Ms. Sc.Brigham Box 5.12.
Honolulu, HI: Bishop Museum.

Brigham, William Tufts. Report on a Journey Around
the World to Study Matters Relating to Museums.
Honolulu, HI: Bishop Museum Press, 1913.

"Brigham Will Now on File For Probate." *Honolulu
Advertiser*, February 5, 1926.

Buckland, Raymond. Buckland's Complete Book of
Witchcraft. St. Paul, MN: Llewellyn Publications,
1999.

Chopra, Deepak, M.D. Quantum Healing: Exploring
the Frontiers of Mind/Body Medicine. New York:
Bantam Books, 1989.

Chun, Malcolm Naea. The History of Licensing
Traditional Native Practitioners. Honolulu, HI: E Ola
Mau, Inc., The Hawaii State Department of Health,
1989.

Claigh, Roberleigh H. The Kahuna Way to Create the
Future in 5 Steps. Koloa, HI: Living Wellness, 1998.

Comeau, Rosalin Uphus. Kamehameha V: Lot
Kapuaiwa. Honolulu, HI: Kamehameha Schools Press,
1996.

Comeau, Rosalin Uphus. Kamehameha The Great.

Cox, J. Halley and Edward Stasack. <u>Hawaiian Petroglyphs</u>. Honoulu, HI: Bishop Museum Press, 1970.

Crif, M. <u>Avava Amkanik Direhma</u>. Amazigh-Voice.com, 2002.

Cunningham, Scott. <u>Hawaiian Magic and Spirituality</u>. St. Paul, MN: Llewellyn Publications, 1994, 2000.

Davis, Eleanor Harmon. <u>Abraham Fornander: A Biography</u>. Honolulu, HI: Univeristy Press of Hawaii, 1979.

"Diamond Head," <u>The New Encyclopaedia Britannica: Macropaedia</u>. 15th ed. Chicago: University Press, 1975.

Elbert, Samuel. <u>Selections from Fornander's Hawaiian Antiquities and Folk Lore</u>. Honolulu, HI: University of Hawaii Press, 1959.

Enomoto, Kekoa Catherine. <u>A Pocket Guide to the Islands—Flowers and Lei</u>. Aiea, HI: Island Heritage Publishing, 1998.

Enomoto, Kekoa Catherine. <u>A Pocket Guide to the Islands—Foods and Flavors</u>. Aiea, HI: Island Heritage Publishing, 1998.

Enomoto, Kekoa Catherine. <u>A Pocket Guide to the Islands—Hula and Chant</u>. Aiea, HI: Island Heritage Publishing, 1998.

Enomoto, Kekoa Catherine. <u>A Pocket Guide to the Islands—Their Songs, Flowers and Colors</u>. Aiea, HI: Island Heritage Publishing, 1998.

Enomoto, Kekoa Catherine. <u>A Pocket Guide to the Islands—Wonderful but Little Known Places</u>. Aiea, HI: Island Heritage Publishing, 1998.

Fornander, Abraham. <u>An Account of the Polynesian Race; Its Origins and Migrations</u>. 1877. Reprinted Rutland, Vermont: Charles E. Tuttle, 1969.

Fornander, Abraham. <u>Collection of Hawaiian Antiquities and Folklore</u>. Honolulu, HI: Bishop Museum, 1916-1919.

Gibaldi, Joseph. <u>MLA Handbook for Writers of Research Papers: 4<u>th</u> Edition</u>. New York: The Modern Language Association, 1995.

Gregory, Herbert E. <u>Report of the Director for 1920</u>. Honolulu, HI: Bishop Press 1921.

Gregory, Herbert E. <u>Report of the Director for 1921</u>. Honolulu, HI: Bishop Press 1922.

Gregory, Herbert E. <u>Report of the Director for 1922</u>. Honolulu: HI, Bishop Press 1923.

Gregory, Herbert E. <u>Report of the Director for 1923</u>. Honolulu, HI: Bishop Press 1924.

Gregory, Herbert E. <u>Report of the Director for 1924</u>. Honolulu, HI: Bishop Press 1925.

Bibliography

Gregory, Herbert E. Report of the Director for 1925. Honolulu, HI: Bishop Press 1926.

Gregory, Herbert E. Report of the Director for 1926. Honolulu, HI: Bishop Press 1927.

Gutmanis, Jane and Theodore Kelsey. Kahuna La'au Lapa'au. Aiea, HI: Island Heritage Publishing, 1976.

Gutmanis, Jane. Na Pule Kahiko: Ancient Hawaiian Prayers. Honolulu, HI: Editions Limited, 1983.

"Hawaii." The New Encyclopaedia Britannica: Macropaedia. 15th ed. Chicago: University Press, 1975.

"Hawaiian Colony in California Gathers to Hear Winona Kanahele." *Honolulu Star Bulletin*, June 1, 1948.

Hoffman, Enid. Huna: A Beginner's Guide. Rockport, MA: Para Research, Inc., 1976.

James Tad, and Ardie James. Lost Secrets of Ancient Hawaiian Huna. Honolulu, HI: Ka Ha O Hawaii Foundation, 1993, 1994.

Johnson, Rubilite Kawena. Kumulipo: Hawaiian Hymn of Creation. Honolulu: HI: Topgallant Publishing Co., LTD, 1981.

Judd, Bernice and Audrey B. Sexton. Missionary Album: Portraits and Biographical Sketches of the American Protestant Missionaries to the Hawaiian Islands. Honolulu, HI: Hawaiian Mission Children's Society, 1969.

"Kahunas Had Something." *The Honolulu Advertiser,* C2, p.. 14, November 27, 1948.

Kalakaua, King David. The Legends and Myths of Hawaii. Honolulu, HI: Mutual Publishing, 1990.

Kamakau, Samuel Manaiakalani. Ka Po'e Kahiko: The People of Old. Honolulu, HI: The Bishop Museum Press, 1991.

Kamakau, Samuel Manaiakalani. Na Hana a ka Po'e Kahiko: The Works of the People of Old. Honolulu, HI: Bishop Museum Press, 1976.

Kelsey, Theodore. Kelsey's Correspondence 1912-1963: Private Collection, M 86, Folder 10: Max Freedom Long. State of Hawaii Archives, 1936, 1940-1941.

Kenn, Charles W. Firewalking from the Inside. Los Angeles, CA: Franklin Thomas, 1949.

Krauss, Bob. "Bishop's First Director Wasn't Exactly 'Mr. Popularity.'" *Honolulu Advertiser*, January 7, 1990.

"Lanai Horror," *The Friend*, Volume 50, Number 7, Honolulu, July, 1892.

Lee, Georgia, and Edward Stasack. Spirit of Place: Petroglyphs of Hawaii. Los Osos, CA: Easter Island Foundation, Bearsville & Cloud Mountain Presses, 1999.

Lee, Pali J. and John K. Willis. Ho'opono. Honolulu: HI: Night Rainbow Publishing, 1999.

Long, Max Freedom. The Huna Code in Religions. Marina Del Rey, CA: DeVorss & Company, 1965, 1993.

Long, Max Freedom. Psychometric Analysis. Cape Girardeau, MO: Huna Research Publications, 1959.

Long, Max Freedom. Rediscovering the Ancient Magic. Cape Girardeau, MO: Huna Press, 1936, 1978.

Long, Max Freedom. Self-Suggestion. Cape Girardeau, MO: Huna Research Publications, 1958.

Long, Max Freedom. Short Talks on Huna. Cape Girardeau, MO: Huna Press, 1978.

Long, Max Freedom. The Secret Science at Work. Marina Del Rey, CA: DeVorss & Company, 1953, 1995.

Long, Max Freedom. The Secret Science Behind Miracles. Marina Del Ray, CA: DeVorss & Company, 1948, 1976.

Long, Max Freedom. Taped Lectures on Huna. Cape Girardeau, MO: Huna Press, 1999.

Long, Max Freedom. What Jesus Taught in Secret. Marina del Rey, CA: DeVorss & Company, 1983.

McBride, Likeke R. The Kahuna: Versatile Masters of Old Hawaii. Hilo, HI: Petroglyph Press, 1972.

Melody. Love is in the Earth: Laying-on-of-Stones. Wheat Ridge, CO: Earth-Love Publishing House, 1992.

Malo, David. Hawaiian Antiquities: Mo'olelo Hawaii. Honolulu, HI: Bishop Museum Press, 1951.

Mitchell, Donald D. Kilolani. Resource Units in Hawaiian Culture. Honolulu: HI: Kamehameha Schools Press, 1982.

Myss, Caroline, Ph.D. Anatomy of the Spirit. New York: Three Rivers Press, 1996.

Palmer, Albert W. Comments on Secret Science Behind Miracles: July 13, 1953 recorded at Bishop Museum. Los Angeles, CA: Kosmon Press, 1948.

Parsons, Claire D.F., Healing Practices in the South Pacific. Honolulu, HI: University of Hawaii Press, Institute for Polynesian Studies, 1985.

Pukui, Mary Kawena. Na'na' I Ke Kumu Volume I and II. (Look to the Source). Honolulu, HI: Hui Ha'nai Queen Lili'uokalani Children's Center, 1972.

Pukui, Mary Kawena and Samuel H. Elbert. Hawaiian Grammar. Honolulu, HI: University Press of Hawaii, 1979.

Bibliography

Pukui, Mary Kawena and Samuel H. Elbert. New Pocket Hawaiian Dictionary. Honolulu, HI: University of Hawaii Press, 1975, 1992.

Roman, Sanaya and Duane Packer. Opening to Channel: How to Connect with Your Guide. Tiburon, CA: H.J. Kramer, Inc., 1987.

Rose, Roger G. A Museum to Instruct and Delight. Honolulu, HI: Bishop Museum Press, 1980.

Schutz, Albert J. All About Hawaiian. Honolulu, HI: University of Hawaii Press, 1995.

Smith, Jonathan Z. and William Scott Green. The Harper Collins Dictionary of Religion. New York, NY: Harper Collins Publishing, 1995.

Steiger, Brad. Kahuna Magic. West Chester, PA: Whitford Press, 1971.

Stein, Diane. Essential Reiki: A Complete Guide to an Ancient Healing Art. Freedom, CA: The Crossing Press, Inc., 1995.

Stokes, John F. G. Report of the Director for 1918. Honolulu, HI: Bishop Press 1919.

Stokes, John F. G. Report of the Director for 1919. Honolulu, HI: Bishop Press 1920.

Waters, Paul. The Adventurer's Quest: Discovering the Ancient Powers of Hawaiian Healing. Princeville, HI: Huna By Mail, 2000.

"William Tufts Brigham Dies After Stroke." *Honolulu Advertiser*, January 30, 1926.

Willis, Koko and Pali Jae Lee. Tales from the Night Rainbow. Honolulu, HI: Night Rainbow Publishing, 1990.

Wilson, Colin. The Psychic Detectives. San Francisco: Mercury House Incorporated, 1985.

Wingo, E. Otha, Ph.D., "The Healing Science of Jesus," The Huna Research Bulletin. June 2001, No. 2.

Yardley, Laura Kealoha. The Heart of Huna. Honolulu, HI: Advanced Neuro Dynamics, Inc., 1982.

Recommended Reading

I would like to recommend a couple of books to those who may wish to read more.

First, *Hawaiian Magic and Spirituality* by the late Scott Cunningham (available through Llewellyn) is in my opinion, the *very best* book on the subject of the actual spiritual practices of Hawaiians. It has a simple, easy to follow format and Cunningham does an excellent job of taking the complex and breaking it down into bite sized pieces. It is a great book! When I was in Honolulu, the staff of Native Books also gave it an endorsement as one of, if not the best book to read, which is significant for Cunningham, who was a non-Hawaiian.

Second, and most obvious, if the previous writing has stirred curiosity about Max Freedom Long's work, I recommend *The Secret Science Behind Miracles*, which is available through DeVorss Publications. If you want the big picture all under one cover of most of Long's theories, this is the book to get. I must say I find the writing a bit tedious at times, yet the information is interesting.

For a more in-depth look at the Hawaiian culture, there are several books listed in the bibliography which are excellent resources. Many are extremely scholarly in nature, yet worth the read. For more specific information, I suggest you contact Native Books or visit their website at www.nativebookshawaii.com.

Index

conscious mind 32
Cook, Captain James 39

D

deities 31
Dole, Stanford B. 47

E

Egypt 51, 64, 106, 137-138
etheric double 58-59, 64, 131

F

Friend, The 46

G

Gospels 52, 63-64

H

Ha (Breath) 57, 130
Haleakala Crater National Park 81
Hana Highway 81
heiau 38, 86, 89, 90-94, 135
Hewahewa 43-45
Hi'aka 34
higher self 32, 55-57, 63, 70-71, 122, 129
Hina 34
Honolulu 47
ho'oponopono 61
Hula 34, 47, 98
Huna Code in Religions *52*
Huna Research Associates 53, 68, 102, 106, 117

I

Iao Needle 79
India 47, 51-52, 56, 64, 139